Goya

and his times

Self-portrait of Goya, about 1795.
Wash drawing in India ink.
The Metropolitan Museum of Art, New York Dick Fund.

Immortals of Art

Goya
and his times

by Monroe Stearns

Franklin Watts, Inc.
575 Lexington Avenue
New York, N.Y. 10022

Front cover: Self-portrait showing Goya's painting habits.
Collection of the Conde de Villagonzalo, Madrid.

PHOTO MAS, BARCELONA

FIRST PRINTING
Library of Congress Catalog Card Number: 66–12123
Copyright © 1966 by Franklin Watts, Inc.
Printed in the United States of America
by Polygraphic Company of America
1 2 3 4 5

To Michael

Contents

List of Illustrations

LIST OF ILLUSTRATIONS

Goya Today

There is a curious parallel between the Spain of the 1760's and the Spain of the 1960's. Two hundred years ago, when Goya first moved from the backwash into the main current of Spanish life, his country was striving to reestablish itself in the community of nations politically, economically, and artistically. In 1964, possibly the most beautiful exhibit at the New York World's Fair was the Pavilion of Spain, designed to reacquaint the world with a country that had been somewhat isolated from contemporary consciousness for the previous thirty-odd years.

Perhaps the greatest of its treasures Spain displayed in that pavilion were five Goyas: *The Naked Maja; The Clothed Maja;* a portrait of Queen Maria Luisa; and two religious subjects, *The Death of St. Joseph* and *St. Bernard and St. Robert* from Valladolid. Later that year F. J. Sánchez Cantón's monumental volume on Goya, with superb color reproductions of Goya's most "modern" work, was published to an enthusiastic reception by the public and critics. It would appear that Spain's bid for new recognition was inseparably connected with Goya, as if he could speak best for the nation and the people he had interpreted with encyclopedic and loving understanding.

Generally speaking, the Spain Goya knew did not appreciate him. He knew it too well for its own comfort, spoke too truly for it to relish what he had to say. His technical

I

achievements, of course, won him fame and respect. They still do. An artist's mastery of his materials, however, is only half his worth. It is his use of them to create enduring symbols that raises him to the ranks of the immortals. Only as his symbols continue to express his perception of the permanent values of man in relation to his world is the artist capable of speaking loudly and clearly enough to be heard across the centuries. The later twentieth century not only can but is willing and eager to hear the message to which Goya's contemporaries were deaf.

Goya was probably the first painter to perceive the iceberg quality of man's nature and existence. Once he had glimpsed the menace of its submerged two-thirds, he could not be content with depicting the glitter of the obvious superstructure. Having recognized this tragic aspect of the human condition, he himself became ennobled by the dignity, the pity, and the hope that a sense of the tragic confers. Let us peer together beneath the surface, Goya says, to observe and study the ballast of our lives.

In his early, purely decorative work, Goya painted the popular games of Spain. Girls toss a manikin in a blanket. Men walk precariously on stilts. A blindfolded girl designates a victim with a wooden spoon. Boys play at fighting a wickerwork "bull." Then Goya sensed that beneath these harmless pastimes lay a cruel parody of man's estate. He restudied them in the light of truth; that is, in a recognition of man's ability to be not the victim but the master of his fate. He transformed the symbols from comedy to tragedy. Life is not a game to be played in fancy clothes and depicted in bright colors. The true colors are somber in the drama of man against the bull—the only animal that attacks without provocation, the symbol of the evil each man must fight alone.

This is what Goya ultimately means by reason. It is the

2

positive life force he would awake to combat the negations
its sleep empowers—superstition, oppression, injustice,
cruelty. He is striving to rid man of his subjection to a
power man thinks is outside himself. He wants man to
understand that he will be free only when he has put his
trust in his perfectibility through his own efforts and
works toward that. The moment of truth arrives when man
alone faces his enemy alone and plunges the sword of
reason straight into the vulnerable hump of the bull of evil.

Goya's genius lies in his creation of a world in which all
this seems possible and plausible. He has, as it were, inverted the iceberg. He has made the invisible apparent.
Life, as Goya pictures it, loses a part of its mystery. Man
stumbles less along its not-so-dark road.

These attitudes, a part of later twentieth-century thinking, were new to Goya's world, which was just beginning
to discover that there is no immutable law of the universe
elevating one man or one class above another. To express
them in pictorial terms Goya recognized that he needed
new techniques, if not a whole new approach to painting.
Consequently, he developed a bold, free brushwork to express his ideals of liberty and democracy. His colors became
the colors of nature, which the eighteenth-century thinkers
interpreted as the reasonable nature of man. Hence, Goya's
tones grew disciplined, so as to stimulate a response from
the reasonable spectator. They involve him actively and
independently in the thinking of the painting, not impose
upon him the artist's will. Delimiting lines disappeared in
Goya's designs to become forms constructed of light and
shade. Similarly, particularizing details vanished, to be
replaced with abstracted essences. In portraits the emphasis was on the human personality of the subject. Every
thing else—even an accurate likeness—was subordinated
to that or omitted entirely.

In both thinking and technique, therefore, Goya pointed the way to realism and impressionism in painting, as those approaches to pictorial communication were developed by Courbet, Manet, van Gogh, Cézanne, and Renoir. It is thus safe to say that Goya was the father of the "modern" style of painting which dominated art from roughly 1850 to 1920. As Goya had learned from Velázquez, Rembrandt, Tiepolo, and El Greco, almost all painters during the century following Goya's death learned from him. Without the tremendous advance into new dimensions of pictorial expression that are represented in Goya's work during his last thirty years, the progress of art might have lagged behind that of such other aspects of civilization as political philosophy, theology, and humanitarianism. Pictures are the most rapid form of communication for ideas. They must keep pace with other expressions of man's adjustment to a world that changes faster now than even Goya recognized it doing during his lifetime. Goya equated the speeds of the two.

This biography aims to give the reader as many significant facts of Goya's life and times as is possible within its compass. The author has tried to interpret these objectively, and to discard or disregard the many improbable legends connected with Goya's life. An obstacle to this intention is the fact that Goya's letters, as well as other documents bearing on his career, have been impounded for twenty-odd years by the Spanish government in order that a definitive edition of them may be compiled. The present author has, therefore, had to rely on the transcripts other biographers and historians have made of these papers.

Goya was not a trained writer or a voluminous one. His language and syntax often suggest more than one interpretation of his intention. It is not clear, for example, whether one of Goya's letters to Martin Zapater refers to the death of Goya's sister or to that of Zapater's. Naturally, translations of the texts vary. The present author has sometimes ventured his own, but more often has followed that of his eminent predecessors.

Readers of other biographies of Goya may notice discrepancies in facts and particularly in dates between those works and this one. Recent investigations reveal lamentable inaccuracies and illogical deductions in several of these works. The present author has taken as his final arbiters the advice of Dr. F. J. Sánchez Cantón and Miss Elizabeth du Gué Trapier, whose researches in depth are both the most recent and the most apparently reliable.

Goya's works hang in public museums and private collections that stretch from Buenos Aires to Budapest. There exist about five hundred of his paintings alone, of which some three hundred are portraits, plus hundreds of drawings and engravings. An accurate count is still impossible owing to problems of location and authentication. It is doubtful that any living writer on Goya has seen all these works; certainly the present author has not. He wishes here to state, without particularizing, that several of his descriptions of individual works have had to be made from reproductions and the analyses of critics. Since this biography is intended primarily for American readers, the author has stressed the works of Goya in America when such examples illustrate trends in Goya's work.

Unfortunately, there are few of Goya's paintings other than portraits in America. The vast majority and by far the greatest of the non-portraits are in the Prado Museum and other galleries in Madrid. With the notable exception of Goya's frescoes in San Antonio de la Florida, in Madrid, Goya's works in other churches of Spain are often so badly lit as to be practically invisible, or are in indifferent states of preservation. Since they seldom represent Goya at his best, they are of true interest only to the specialist.

The layman can get a more than adequate acquaintance with Goya's work by visiting the three repositories mentioned above, and these others: the Metropolitan Museum of Art, the Frick Collection, and the Hispanic Society of America, in New York City; the National Gallery of Art, Washington, D. C.; the Art Institute of Chicago. A few outstanding works are in the National Gallery of Art, London; the Louvre, Paris; the Museum of Fine Arts, Agen, France; the Museum of Fine Arts, Castres, France. Prints of Goya's etchings and lithographs are in several representative museums and, along with many of his drawings, have been well reproduced in books listed in the bibliography of this volume. It is not so essential for anyone but the specialist to study these engravings at first hand as it is for him to see the paintings themselves.

The author warmly thanks Miss Elizabeth du Gué Trapier and the library staff of the Hispanic Society of America for their cooperation and help, and all the private owners of Goyas who have graciously permitted visits to their homes.

MONROE STEARNS

New York, N. Y.

1

The Colors of Aragon

A small parade of peasants marched down the one street—if indeed it could be called that—of a hamlet in north central Spain one early spring morning in 1746. The beams of the young sun bounced off whitewashed walls on to the buff dust of the road, narrowing eyes, deepening lines in faces of crackled parchment. The women wore black as they had done since the days of the Moors. Black shawls shrouded their hair. Black broad-brimmed, low-crowned hats sat low on the heads of the men. Their shoulders bulged under short black jackets above yellowish leather breeches. Stocky legs swelled their white wool stockings.

It was no unusual occasion, this trip up the steep hill to the parish Church of the Assumption for the baptism of a new baby. Yet most of the hundred-odd souls who inhabited Fuendetodos came to their doorway to watch, crossed themselves, and murmured a prayer for the survival of the infant. Far too many of the babes born in that isolated spot did not live to grow up. They needed protection in every way possible from the Devil and his hosts that infested the earth.

The priest took the day-old baby from the arms of his godmother, Francisca Grasa, and mumbled the ritual of the sacrament. Then, the ceremony over, the clerk of the parish made a lengthy entry in the registry to the effect that the newborn son of Francisco de Paula José Goya and the former Gracia (or Engracia) Lucientes had been born on Wednesday, March 30, 1746, and was now a child of God. Several other saints' names were also given the infant, for each saint so honored would lend protection. But he was to be known thereafter only as Francisco José Goya y Lucientes.

Then the christening party descended the hill to celebrate the event at José Goya's house in the lower part of the town, at 15, Calle de la Alhóndiga.

Possibly the feasting was a little more elaborate than customary in that poverty-ridden settlement. Gracia Goya claimed to be an *hidalga*, one of the hundreds of thousands of Spaniards who traced their descent from some provincial landowner. Thus she had inherited a pride that made even the thought of manual work distasteful.

The house had belonged to Gracia's family. Its thick walls of unevenly set stones still stand under a tiled roof. A step down from the street level leads to a large room with a roughhewn beamed ceiling. There two stone benches flank a large fireplace. Beyond is a smaller, stone-walled room, the kitchen. Above the larger room is another, lit by a heavily shuttered, unglazed window. There Gracia was recovering from her delivery. Over the

Goya's birthplace, Fuendetodos, Spain.
PHOTO MAS, BARCELONA

kitchen a dark storeroom with a slanting roof held the family's provisions of sausages, bunches of onions, piles of grain. That was all. The house is scarcely more than a peasant's hut.

José Goya was a peasant with a trade; that is, he was considered better than a common laborer. In Zaragoza, the capital of the province of Aragon, some thirty-five miles to the northeast, he had worked as a gilder, making picture frames and applying gold leaf to them, religious statues and furniture. Apparently he did not prosper. Spanish art and decoration had barely begun again to flourish under the then king of Spain, the melancholy Philip V.

After his lucky marriage, José moved to Fuendetodos to occupy the house and land his wife's dowry had brought him. With his own hands he worked the fields just beyond the hamlet.

Three years after the birth of Francisco, José Goya went back to Zaragoza. There the Cathedral of the Virgin of the Pillar (*El Pilar*) was nearing completion. Gilt-work was needed for its rococo design. José could make a better living by his trade than by tilling the stony fields around Fuendetodos.

Soon he owned a house in Zaragoza, in the Calle de la Morería Cerrada, the old Moorish quarter of the city. Later he moved to the Calle de Rufas. He brought his family there when he felt he could afford to educate his children. By then there were three more: Camillo, who became a priest; Tomás, who became a gilder like his father; Rita, who married a Zaragozan and died at about the age of thirty. There seem to have been two other children, an older boy and a girl, who died in infancy.

Very little more is known about José and Gracia Goya. José, the son of a notary, had come down in the world, but he was ambitious for his children; he is said to have sold the Zaragoza house to provide for Francisco's education. From him the painter might have got the peasant shrewdness which never left him, a certain wry humor, and a way of learning about life from life itself.

Furthermore, the father's work with art objects brought the boy into touch with paintings and sculpture and with those who created them. Perhaps young Francisco was first stimulated to express his private vision of the world by a wish to imitate his father's patrons. There were plenty of men practicing art in Zaragoza then, however uninspired their products were. The Aragonese school of art had been moribund for four hundred years.

Much of his childhood Francisco spent in the country, as a peasant among peasants. Fuendetodos, which today numbers about three hundred inhabitants, was an outpost in a land of ocher-colored soil and dry vegetation. Cold winds from the north shriveled the people and changed them quickly from youth to old age. In the village, the hovels still center around the church, a humble monument to the Catholic faith. In the fields a tree is a rarity. The sky is silent and cloudless. A stream, the Huerva, creeps by. Fuendetodos nestles at the foot of heather-covered mountains topped with black pines. These were the colors Goya first knew and always remembered: black, yellow, white, cold blue.

In this elemental setting the boy learned the forms and tones of nature. He also learned to know people at their simplest, for his family lived as plainly as had their ancestors. At home, life centered around the fireplace, the only source of warmth and light in the house. In the remote corners of the rooms the dark, heavy furniture glinted like spectral forms. There lurked witches and goblins like those which peopled the stories superstitious, almost illiterate Gracia Goya told her children.

The boy grew stocky and strong. Those who recalled him much later said he was a sad-faced child who talked little and seemed to live in a world of his own. Perhaps he heard only a bit of what was said to him or of what went on around him; he had earaches. His former neighbors said he liked to be alone in the fields and the mountains, and that he would make pictures of the weird faces he saw in gnarled tree trunks and in stones and clouds.

In church he would stare at the gargoyles and the gothic monsters, which symbolized the ever present power of evil. The religion he learned was elemental, requiring only pious conduct. It served him the rest of his life. At least once he admitted feeling guilty at his non-Christian conduct and the persistence of his sin of pride. He took religion literally and perhaps superstitiously, for he always marked his letters with a cross. Later he described his wife and himself as "firmly believing and confessing the mystery of the Holy Trinity . . . and all other mysteries and sacraments believed and confirmed by our Holy Roman Catholic Apostolic Church, in whose true faith and belief we have lived." He seems not to have speculated much about the meanings of those mysteries, or even to have understood them. He had no use for those who retreated from life in the hope of finding its significance.

The pain of his earaches and the isolation they inflicted made Francisco rebellious. They were the aggressive evil he had to fight against, an undeserved punishment from a hostile God. He grew pugnacious and stubborn. He would fly into a rage at a word or an action without thinking of what it truly meant or of the effect of his behavior on others. He would not let his slightest whim be blocked. Nothing was to hinder his battle for the place in the world he felt was unfairly denied him.

His affliction made him his mother's pet. His father took

11

great pride in the boy's sensitive responses. Francisco loved them both, treated them with affection and generosity, referred to them humorously as *los viejos* (the old folks), grieved when they died. His battle was not against people but against the unjust powers of the universe.

The Aragonese has to rely on himself. His roots are in a hard land. Their fruit is pride and stubbornness—rebellion against grim, uncompromising forces that must be subdued.

With a desert climate, Spain has many regions that are almost desert. Aragon is one of them, lacking water, pastureland, trees. It bears the scars of ancient wars. Ruins of Moorish fortresses cap the hills; there was one near Fuendetodos. Zaragoza, the capital of Aragon, is a forbidding city that concentrates the spirit of its region—firm, hard, independent, and unselfconscious; energetic, forceful, imaginative. It is also a sinister city, fit to be the scene of Verdi's romantic opera, *Il Trovatore*. The palace of that drama's Count di Luna, now the Audiencia, with its figures of half-naked ogres carrying clubs, probably scared young Goya. Zaragoza's famous leaning tower was razed in 1877.

Francisco went to live there more or less permanently when he was about eight years old. Since his own father had been an educated man, José Goya wanted his son to be one also. Thus Francisco might redeem the family name from the low esteem to which José had brought it. The boy had shown he was intelligent enough to warrant a formal education. He was put in the Escuela Pía de San Antonio in Zaragoza, which was presided over by a Father Joaquin.

The experience was a grim one for Francisco Goya. School discipline was severe. The switch was in constant use, for it was firmly believed that learning stuck best when it had been beaten in. All instruction was based on religion and patriotism, which were considered enough to make an ideal Spanish citizen.

More attention was being paid to education, however, in the latter half of the eighteenth century than previously. It had finally been acknowledged that the proper training of children is an essential for a strong nation of men.

The ideal curriculum was reading and writing and Castilian pronunciation at age eight, followed the next year by arithmetic, algebra, and geometry. Geography occupied the student's third year of study. For the next two years he was to learn religious and secular history, after which came two years of foreign languages.

Probably no one school realized that ideal. Only some four hundred thousand of Spain's three and a half million children were educated at all in its fifteen hundred-odd schools.

Whatever Goya may have learned in Father Joaquin's school—he seems to have acquired a proficiency in mathematics, but he never mastered spelling—was of little importance to his later life in comparison with the fact that there he met Martín Zapater y Clavería. They remained lifelong friends. Almost all of what is truly known about Goya's inner life is derived from the 135 letters he wrote to Zapater during a forty-year period. Many of the events of Goya's life and many of the pictures he painted can be dated accurately through this affectionate correspondence. Zapater's letters to Goya have disappeared, but he kept all of the painter's.

The two had little in common except that both were peasants from the same region. Zapater lived all his life in the provincial capital, and seems to have been a conservative man, though not without imagination. He was of a good family, and later he was one of Zaragoza's most influential citizens. Having become a rich bourgeois through furnishing supplies to the army, he acted as Goya's investment counselor, giving him good advice and sometimes even lending him money.

Martín Zapater was more to young Francisco Goya than just a school chum. The gilder's son was beginning to find himself different from his colleagues, more sensitive to what he saw and felt, choked with reactions he had to cough out or strangle. The physical energy he had built up in the freedom of the fields and the mountains demanded release. Sensing himself an individual, and an original one at that, he craved another human being who would listen, understand, respond. "The good Martín," as Goya was to address him, served his purpose and posterity simply by being there.

All of Goya's turbulent egoism was mirrored in Zapater's stolidity. Goya loved the reflection of himself he saw in the one person of his own age whose affection expanded that image to completion. Actually, he got from Zapater more than he gave. "Martín of my soul," he would write, as if to acknowledge that debt, "I know we understand each other in every respect. God made us to do so. Let us be heartily thankful to Him for that."

After school hours Francisco could linger around the studios of the painters and artisans who were his father's clients. He was fascinated by the facility with which they transformed ideas into pictorial form. It is likely that he himself began working backward, as it were, from what he saw to what he felt; then forward, as these painters seemed to be doing, from what he felt to what he could see. The process put his feelings into better order. He began to understand himself. He felt less isolated as he saw his private vision of the world—the way he himself felt and thought about things—accepted and shared by others.

On a visit to Fuendetodos he found the church where he had been baptized pathetically bare of any decoration like that which was being lavished on the Cathedral of El Pilar in Zaragoza. It pained him. He offered to paint draperies over and around the niche above the altar in which the relics of the church were ranged like wares in a china shop. Permission was granted, and the boy went to work.

The work perished during the Spanish Civil War. Photographs taken before 1936 show it to have been no more than could be expected of a twelve- or thirteen-year-old boy. It was stiff, conventional, and imitative of the Zaragozan painters, who themselves were imitators of decadent Italians.

The story goes that as Goya was working on the decoration of the Church of the Assumption, the feudal overlord of Fuendetodos paid a visit to the church. This was the Count of Fuentes, a member of the Pignatelli family, which was of Neapolitan origin. Rich and influential, he was a patron of the arts and of artists. Seeing that, however crude Goya's work was, the young painter had promise, the Count undertook to pay for Goya's education in art, and had the boy sent to José Luzán y Martinez, whose artistic training the Count had also financed.

Goya's first work, the "curtains" of the altarpiece in the parish church of Fuendetodos.
PHOTO MAS, BARCELONA

It is clear that Goya knew the Fuentes family, and profited from the acquaintance. José Goya, however, could easily have recognized his son's aptitude. Francisco apparently was always drawing or painting, much as a child who adores music darts compulsively to any instrument whatever. Such dedication is a sign of genius. Many artists, even when mature, cannot keep from sketching on whatever material is handy, no matter what the circumstances. It is their way of "verbalizing" their ideas. They tend to think in forms rather than in words. One line leads to another until a pictorial concept is reached. Similarly, a composer thinks in terms of sound. A more verbally minded person thinks in words, but pictorial and musical artists are often rather inarticulate.

Thanks to his clients, José Goya could also have arranged for Francisco's training in art. At any rate, when the boy was about fourteen years old and had completed his formal schooling, he entered Luzán's studio. There were other students, among them Beraton, Tomás Vallespin, and Antonio Martínez, all of whom became well-known painters in Aragon.

Luzán had been born in Zaragoza about 1710. The Pignatelli family had sent him to Italy, where he studied in Naples under Nicolo Mastroleo (d. 1744), a painter of historical subjects in the manner of Luca Giordano (1632–1705). Giordano was well known to art-conscious Spaniards, for he had painted frescoes in the Escorial in Spain during the late seventeenth century.

The first influence on the style of the person who was to become probably the greatest of Spanish painters—and certainly the greatest interpreter of Spain—was, therefore, not Spanish. Since the death of Diego Velázquez (1599–1660), and of his son-in-law and principal follower, Juan del Mazo (c. 1612–77), no Spanish painter had reached the high level of art Velázquez set. Furthermore, when the Bourbons succeeded to the throne of Spain in 1700, they favored the French and Italian styles to which they were accustomed. The Spanish style, which had expressed the Spanish temperament, succumbed to importations. The Neapolitan tradition, being popular with the sovereigns, was transplanted into Spain.

Of all the styles in the history of art, this rococo is the least appealing to a modern taste. It was a weak imitation of the masters of the Italian Renaissance and baroque period. It aimed at being decorative, not at interpreting nature or human life. Ornament had replaced simplicity and directness. Movement had become agitation. Inspiration came from romances and chronicles, not from life itself. Formalism was substituted for originality of composition. The pictures often covered acres and included hundreds of supposedly human figures posed either like clothing dummies—the nearest the painters could come to reproducing the restraint of classical sculpture—or in spasms of religious hysteria.

Giordano, called "the Speedy," possibly the best of these decadent painters, left an incredible number of works in Spain and elsewhere in Europe. They were widely imitated by other workers, few of whom approached Giordano's inventiveness and occasional charm. José Luzán y Martínez was one of these.

Nevertheless, when Luzán returned from Italy to Zaragoza in 1735, he gradually acquired a lucrative reputation among the Church authorities on art in northern Spain. He was made Court Painter to Philip V in 1744, and artistic censor of the Inquisition, which ruled on all matters of religion in Spain. He was a cultured man, but a plodding, painstaking, provincial one.

Luzán is said to have been a good teacher, who did not

charge his pupils fees. His credo, at least, was that in order
to reach perfection in art, one must teach it—a theory with
which more-inspired artists rarely agree; Goya himself did
little if any teaching. But the Prado, the magnificent national gallery of Spain and one of the world's greatest
museums, has never seen fit to include any of Luzán's
sweet coloring in its collections.

Luzán had a large collection of engravings of works by
master painters and a number of plaster casts of antique
statues that he had brought from Italy. Goya was set to
copying these copies. It was a dull curriculum. In the long
run it did Goya little good. Accurate draughtsmanship
was never one of his major achievements. Although he was
to produce some of the world's most imaginative and spirited drawings, it was only after he had discarded the tight,
hard lines Luzán and Goya's other teachers insisted on.

In a brief memoir of his father, Goya's son Javier wrote:
"He was a pupil of Don José Luzán in Zaragoza . . . for
four years, during which he was prevented from painting
according to his own invention."

Repressed in Luzán's workshop, Goya found release for
his energies in the life of Zaragoza. The city was ugly, but
it was not torpid. Writing of a visit he made there a few
years later, that indefatigable traveler, lover, and diarist,
Giovanni Jacopo Casanova, remarked that "the bullfights
were finer in Zaragoza than in Madrid—that is to say, they
were deadlier . . ." Goya was as involved in them as any
typical American boy of today is in baseball.

For centuries bullfighting in Spain had been the prerog-
ative of the nobles. Then Philip V, the first Bourbon king
of Spain, not being a Spaniard and hence not appreciating
the almost mystic significance of the ritual to his subjects,
turned bullfighting over to the populace on the grounds
that it was too barbaric a diversion for his courtiers. If he

had hoped to abolish it by undignifying it, his dreams were vain. The Spanish people quickly changed it into an art to be practiced only by professionals. By the middle of the eighteenth century these *toreros* were the heroes of the people and the darlings of noble ladies.

The competition among the fighters led them to invent feats of agility and bravery in the ring, some of which became as standard in a performance as, say, an *entrechat* in a ballet. Fighting the bull on horseback (*rejón*), as the nobles had done, waned in popularity. (It is still performed, but as a diversion, particularly in Mexico and Portugal, simply to arouse the bull; the killing is done on foot.) Francisco Romero, one of the greatest of *toreros*, invented killing the bull face to face after provoking it with a cape or *muleta*. Pepe Costillares introduced the *volapié* —a half-running, half-flying attack—and initiated the now-typical costume of pink stockings, tight and brightly colored breeches, gorgeously embroidered short jacket, pigtail, and two-cornered hat. Pedro Romero, Francisco's grandson, developed the elegant, confident style of Rondera. His rival, the extraordinarily handsome José Delgado (Pepe Hillo), countered with the Sevillan style of slender, small-featured fighters with graceful, nimble footwork. After Juan Romero organized professionals into teams, called *cuadrillas*, every Spanish boy dreamed of joining one.

Until they were old enough to do so, the boys played at bullfighting in the streets. One would cover his head with a wicker basket shaped like a bull, while others, mounted on their playmates' shoulders, would try to overturn him with long sticks. Goya undoubtedly played in these sand-lot *corridas* over and over again. He was to make one the subject of a tapestry cartoon, and to parody one in Plate 77 of the *Caprichos*.

Perhaps he himself actually entered the ring, even at this early age. Young boys in Spain still leap over the barrier into the bullring and, before they are chased out, try to display skills acquired through practicing on young bulls in pastures. Charles Poore tells of a twelve-year-old boy who jumped into the ring with homemade equipment during a gala *corrida* in 1932. He won the congratulations of the great Belmonte and an ovation from the crowd before being kicked out. Late in his life Goya told his friend Moratín that he had fought bulls in the arena when young. Perhaps it was only an old man fulfilling a childish wish, perhaps not. There is a legend that he worked his way from Spain to Italy as a member of a traveling *cuadrilla*. At any rate, no one ever loved bullfighting with a greater passion, or had a keener understanding of its mystique, than Francisco Goya.

To the initiate the bullfight is more than a sport. It has a religious significance half as old as time. Its mystery, like any other, has many plausible interpretations. Fundamentally, it symbolizes man's necessity to conquer and destroy in order to survive. At a higher level, it is man versus the force of evil that challenges his hope of salvation. It has been seen as the battle between the sexes, and as the triumph of civilization over barbarism. No *aficionado* can witness the final moment of truth, the single expert thrust, without experiencing a spiritual catharsis. Even at its lowest level of meaning, a bullfight is as graceful and colorful an exhibition of human agility as a classical ballet.

Like any other gifted adolescent of his time, Goya learned to play the national instrument, the guitar. He became expert, for he loved music. Later, whenever he found a new score, he would send it to Martín Zapater in a letter expressing his own enthusiasm for it.

The Moorish traditions had not vanished from Zaragoza nearly four hundred years after those Easterners had been expelled from Spain. The wild wailing of their music still lingers in the national melodies of Spain. It was these that inflamed the hot blood of the young Goya. Moorish in origin also is the custom of the Zaragozans of practically living in the streets, mingling with one another, knowing everyone else. All this brought Goya early familiarity with people and with what makes human nature human. It supplied him with the humor that made him able to detect with deadly accuracy the real person behind the sham, the truth beneath artificiality.

Swordsmanship young Goya learned both for purposes of offense and defense. Casanova described the long cloaks and low hats of the Zaragozans, adding that:

> *They looked like dark phantoms more than men, for the cloak covered up at least half the face. Underneath the cloak was carried* el espadin, *a sword of enormous length. Persons who wore this costume were treated with the greatest respect, though they were mostly arrant rogues; still they might be powerful noblemen in disguise.*

Goya was no powerful nobleman. Whether or not he was an arrant rogue depends on one's faith in the legends that sprang up about him soon after his death. These were purveyed to Goya's early biographers by oldsters who at best could remember him but dimly as a youth. His first biographer, the obscure painter Valentin Cardarera, thought that "if Goya had written his autobiography, it would have been as interesting as that of the famous Benvenuto Cellini." This is undoubtedly an exaggeration. Goya was probably no angel, but his short, barrel-chested, enormously powerful physique, topped by a round face with a snub nose, implies that he was more an outdoor athlete than a bedroom brigand. He was fundamentally too prudent a peasant to indulge in the excesses of the passionate Florentine. Especially in Goya's early years his character seems to have been frank, modest, brave, and natural.

At the age of seventeen, Francisco Goya found that he had learned all the artists of Zaragoza could teach him. He had broadened his instruction by entering the school of design taught by Juan Ramirez, a sculptor, but there again he was compelled to copy. Ramirez had also brought back from Italy plaster casts of ancient sculpture. He set Goya once more to drawing from the antique. There was still no opportunity for Goya to paint "according to his own invention."

Madrid, the capital of Spain, two hundred miles to the southwest, beckoned. There the new monarch Charles III was encouraging the arts. There on the Alcalá near the Plaza Mayor was the Academy of San Fernando, which had been founded in 1752. It offered instruction in the neoclassic style of painting, which was just coming into favor. Francisco Bayeu, another Zaragozan and a former pupil of Luzán's, was thriving in Madrid as a Court Painter.

The ambitious José Goya gave his no-less-ambitious son the equivalent of about one hundred dollars. "My boy," he said, "if you are good, that money can take you to Madrid and Rome."

And so, in 1763, Francisco Goya was off to make his way in the world.

2

The Wander Years

A journey anywhere in Spain was something to be undertaken only out of the most urgent necessity. Conditions of
travel made the chances of arriving safely at one's destination at best even. The roads were little more than mule
tracks and were infested with brigands. It was next to
impossible to travel without being robbed or murdered, as
Goya's several paintings of highway incidents show. There
were as yet no long distance coaches; even when a system
of diligences was inaugurated some twenty years after
Goya's first trip to Madrid, the vehicles were ancient.

Inns along the way were full of vermin and thieves. In
order to rest, one had to spread one's blankets on a floor
black with fleas and stinking with bugs. (Most Spaniards,
for that matter, were crawling with lice. Delousing a friend,
even in public, was considered a favor; there were also
professional delousers. Spaniards rarely bathed. Their tradition of shunning water went back to the time when they
wanted to show their difference from the Moors, who
bathed frequently.)

Just to face such a trip alone, especially for someone
who had never been away from home before, took courage.
But Goya was young and full of bright dreams, and was
strong, and a master swordsman.

By December 4, 1763, he had entered Madrid through

one of the gates in its mud walls. It was a comparatively new city, having been created out of a village only three hundred years before to make a capital in the center of the country.

It was the dirtiest city in Spain and one of the dirtiest in all Europe. There were only four fine streets in it—named Toledo, Atocha, Alcalá, and San Jeronimo. The rest were narrow, winding, steep, paved if at all with stones as sharp as daggers, and deeply covered with refuse, garbage, and slop. Dead horses lay about in them, and pigs and dogs scavenged.

The houses were small and generally of one story, for if there were other floors, the second of them automatically belonged to the king and had to be rented back from him by the owner of the property. Their wooden doors and window frames were dingy for want of paint, and the glass panes were of such poor quality that only a little light filtered into the gloomy dwellings. At night the city was pitch dark. Anyone who had to go about then was wise to be fully armed.

This squalor was being improved as rapidly as the wishes of Charles III, who was disgusted with the conditions, could creep through the tangled bureaucracy of the city administration. The year before Goya arrived, Sacchetti's palace atop Madrid's highest hill had been completed in the Italian-French style of architecture. It was one of the most gorgeous royal residences in the world. When Napoleon saw it, he remarked to his brother Joseph, who was occupying it: "Even I do not live so well as you."

Gradually the dilapidated houses were being replaced by better ones. Public buildings designed by such able architects as Ventura Rodríguez, Juan de Villaneuva, and Sabatini were beginning to rise. The park of the Prado, formerly a dark, evil spot fit only for political and amorous intrigues, was being transformed into a delightful place for the people to amuse themselves with nude bathing, music, and late dancing.

Another park, the Buen Retiro, where there had been a royal residence, was reserved for the aristocracy. Proper dress was obligatory if one wanted to sit in its straw chairs to sip chocolate and gossip, or attend its theater. It was free of the gangs of boys who roamed the Prado, of the Prado's noisy vendors of oranges, chestnuts, and other tidbits, and of its swarms of beggars. Of the approximately one hundred and fifty thousand inhabitants of Madrid then, some thirty thousand were beggars, living on the alms of the charitable and on the bowl of soup distributed to them daily by the Church.

The division between the aristocracy and the populace was equally sharp in other areas. Because of the French origins of the reigning House of Bourbon, French styles and customs were the fashion for the nobility. These had reached a new peak of ornamental artificiality. Anything natural was considered barbarous.

It was an age of lace and satin and powdered hair. Its colors were sentimental blues and pink and gilt. It was the age of Dresden china shepherds and shepherdesses, any one of whom would rather have died than touch a sheep; of mincing gentlemen and coquettish ladies acting out a fancy-dress-ball existence that ignored all realities but those which might contribute to the perfumed pursuit of pleasure. Even the personal mannerisms of the aristocracy followed the injunctions of French dancing masters; hence, the outward-pointed toes, the arch gestures, the cocked little fingers which appear in the poses of the nobles who sat for the unrealistic Court Painters, and even for Goya.

The middle class of Madrid society was ill-defined because of recent royal decrees designed to make work honorable so that anything essential to the nation's existence could be accomplished. For centuries the basic pretension to social prestige had been not to demean oneself by labor. Now edicts declaring that trades are "decent and honorable and that the practice of them in no way degrades the person . . . nor does it prevent his obtaining government employment or attaining the rank of nobility" were gradually taking effect. The middle class, once frivolous and vain and luxury-loving, was becoming an active force in Spanish life.

The important force contrasting with the aristocracy was the lower class, the *manoleria,* who lived in the Lavapié and Avapié sections of Madrid. Dominating it were the *majos* and *majas,* who hated foreign influence in dress, manners, and every other dimension of Spanish life. They stood for the true Spanish customs and character. In the complexity of Madrid society, new and baffling to a young painter from the provinces, this element answered to Goya's own nature. During his early years in Madrid he spent most of his time among these people, the only ones he could find who were truly real. He was to paint them again and again with understanding and respect.

Majos had no highfalutin notions about the indignity of labor. They worked with their hands and were fiercely proud of their trade. They were cobblers, innkeepers and tavern keepers, bakers, and tailors; but above all they were blacksmiths. So popular was that trade among them that the class was also called *chisperos* (from *chispas,* the sparks from their anvils). Their manner was a combination of cold pomposity and menacing severity.

Their outstanding characteristic was their clothes, again a protest against the Frenchification of the Spanish national costume. Above white stockings they wore close-fitting knee breeches designed to show off the shapeliness

26

of their legs and thighs. Their feet were encased in buckled slippers. A short jacket over a gaudy waistcoat ended in a long, wide sash about their waist. Their hair they wore long, caught in a net behind that was tied on top of their head with a ribbon. Over that they would set a round hat, sometimes high-crowned and pointed. Between their teeth would usually be a long black cigar, another contrast to the aristocracy, who took snuff. Over and around everything else they slung a long, full black cape, occasionally worn so as to muffle the face up to the eyes.

Their female counterparts, the *majas,* were no less colorful and fear-inspiring. They were vendors by occupation, selling in the streets the produce they bought from peasant farmers along the highways—everything from parsley to limes and chestnuts. Goya particularly admired the haughty, spirited chestnut vendors and included them in many of his genre scenes. Sometimes the *majas* worked as marketwomen or as servants. They had sharp tongues and an arrogant way of using them. Their language was colorful, and they usually carried out their boastful threats, sometimes with the dagger each wore in a sheath attached to her left garter.

Like the *majos* they took pride in clothes of their own styling, but they generally dressed up only on gala occasions. Then they wore low shoes, a full skirt, a low-necked embroidered bodice, and around their neck a scarf or a small shawl. Their hair was topped by a high comb over which was draped a mantilla. They had their own code of honor and their own rules for dealing with their *majo.* They would exchange gifts with him, and hit him when angry, but they would not fight with him. When together, they would walk down the middle of a street, making room for no one. They epitomized the fierce, independent pride of the Spanish peasant, the backbone of his nation.

Goya came to Madrid at the beginning of a period of

change. It had commenced in 1761 with Charles III's decision to beautify the city, but this was but the first visible symbol of a transformation that would affect the entire nation and country throughout the rest of Goya's life, and him along with it.

The changes did not come about without a struggle. Every Spaniard was taught to have respect for God, the king, and his own family, including himself. The three, once harmonious, soon were to come into conflict with one another.

God, represented by the Church, owned one-sixth of the land of Spain. Its revenues were only slightly less than those of the state. The clergy numbered one hundred and fifty thousand in a total population of about ten million. There were thirty-six different Orders of monks and four military Orders, and thirty thousand nuns belonging to twenty-nine different Orders. The people had tremendous veneration for the sacraments and rituals of the Church. Its religious festivals captured their imagination. True religious feeling, however, had succumbed to ritual, superstition, and politics. It was no longer a force in the life of the people.

The enlightened absolutism of the Bourbon Charles III curbed the power of the Church, which had increased under the previous dynasty, the Hapsburgs, who had to depend on it after they had alienated the middle class. In 1766 the Jesuits were expelled from Spain because of their political intriguing. But the Inquisition still flourished, though its flagrant abuses of what is known as justice in a democracy were somewhat curtailed.

This Gestapo of the Church was concerned with discovering and punishing crimes against religion, principally bigamy, sorcery, and blasphemy. The last was a blanket term for any deviation whatever from what the authorities considered proper or advantageous to Church and state.

The accused was haled before the Court of the Inquisition and charged with his offense. The names of his accusers and of the witnesses against him were withheld from him. The procedure was completely secret. If the accused did not confess, he was urged to do so by torture. Inevitably judged guilty, he was kept in prison until an *auto-da-fé* (act of faith) could be arranged in the Plaza Mayor, the principal square of Madrid.

An auto-da-fé was a public shaming of the victim. The prisoner was dressed in a *sanbenito,* a yellow scapular-shaped garment emblazoned with the red cross of St. Benedict (San Benito). It was also inscribed with the culprit's name, his social condition, his crime, and the date of his conviction. If he was to die at the stake, the garment was of black, and symbols of the flames were substituted for the red cross along with devils and other figures representing his crime. On his head was placed the *coroza,* a cone-shaped cap three feet high, covered with the same material as the sanbenito, and decorated with figures or an inscription detailing the crime and the method of punishment prescribed.

The city authorities and officials gathered in the square to await the arrival of the shaming procession, which had wound through the streets of the city. The records of the Inquisition on the case were read aloud. Then the victim—sometimes many victims—was "released" to the secular arm of the law. The judge condemned the offender to death, and he was executed immediately. The unrepentant were burned alive; the repentant were garroted first, then burned. A few repentant victims were sentenced to the *misericordia* (mercy) prisons of the Inquisition, a fate of debatable preference to the scaffold.

Garroting was the method of execution for common

criminals. These, too, were exposed to public shame, being forced to ride on a mule down the Calle Mayor to the square. Their captors lashed their bare breasts and shoulders while the public crier proclaimed their crime and its punishment. Then, on the scaffold, they were tied on a bench and against a post at their back, and given a crucifix to hold while the public executioner tightened with a screw the iron collar that would strangle them.

All these gruesome scenes Goya was to paint and draw and etch in protest against their barbarity, injustice, and pointlessness.

The king was a father figure to the Spaniards. He was the anointed of God, and he ruled by divine right. Whether he was good or bad, wise or foolish, his office was so sacred that it blinded the Spaniards to the faults of its occupant. "In our Spanish masses," wrote Charles III's minister, Campomanes, "there is no opinion more deeply set than this: the king is absolute lord of the lives, the possessions, and the honor of us all. To put this truth in doubt is held as a kind of sacrilege."

Charles III, who occupied the throne from 1759 to 1788, was one of the best of all Spanish kings. He was meticulous, precise, and hardworking, keeping to a rigorous schedule of activities for each and every day. His remedy for the melancholy that affected his family was constant activity. Intelligent and alert, he was fully aware of his duty to his kingdom. His policies were liberal and rational. And he had the sense to obtain and keep able ministers. The most prominent of these were the Count of Aranda and the Count of Floridablanca, the latter of whom advanced Goya's ambitions. Under Charles III the Court was strict and moral, full of stiff ceremonies and little gaiety. Charles was an abstemious widower who, as he did in Goya's case, often ranked virtue higher than ability.

The king ruled as an absolute monarch. There was a body of nobles, called the *cortes*, which supposedly recommended legislation, but it met only three times during the entire eighteenth century and then acted as a rubber stamp for the proposals of the king and his ministers. Internal affairs were handled by the local cortes in each of the provinces of Spain. These were intended to be responsible to the central cortes. Actually they acted independently and, for the most part, far more judiciously than the principal body.

The individual Spaniard was trapped, though he did not often know it. On the one hand was his own proud independence. On the other was his slavish acceptance of outworn, superstitious tradition and the absolutism of the Church and the government. Yet of all the peasantries of medieval Europe, the Spanish was the most emancipated. Spain was the most democratic country. Because of this tradition of relative freedom, and because of the Spaniard's reverence for his king, a revolution such as would soon erupt in France was unthinkable.

What the Spanish people would not stand was interference from outside. This hatred was to show itself vividly in their resistance to the French invaders of 1808. It was already manifest in their opposition to the French and Italian ministers the Bourbon kings imported from their own homeland. Charles III had been king of Naples before he was summoned to assume the crown of Spain on the death of his half brother, Ferdinand.

An example of this opposition to foreign influence occurred soon after Goya had arrived in Madrid. Since he was a Spaniard through and through, and as yet too inexperienced to see the possible benefits of a less provincial administration, he doubtless took part in the uprising against the decrees of Charles III's Italian minister, Prince Squillaci, or, in Spanish, Esquilache.

31

The symbol of Spanish national dress was the long, full cape and the wide-brimmed slouch hat. A Spaniard would rather have gone barefoot than capeless. But both the cape and the hat fostered crime, the one because it concealed weapons and pilfered articles, the other because it could be pulled over the face, concealing a criminal's identity.

On March 10, 1766, Esquilache decreed that capes and hats must be reduced in size to certain arbitrary measurements. He enforced the order drastically. A contemporary print shows official tailors stationed in doorways and on street corners to trim the garments of those who refused to comply with the new law. Esquilache even went so far as to advise adoption of the French style of coat and stiff three-cornered hat.

This was too much from a foreigner. The Sunday after the order was published, a group of *majos* openly defied it. The police stepped in. A crowd gathered and began chanting: "Long live King Charles! Down with Esquilache!"

Presently a full-fledged riot greeted the king as he was coming back into the city with his eldest son from hunting. Terrified by such unheard-of behavior on the part of his hitherto loyal and obedient subjects, he fled by night to his palace at Aranjuez, about twenty-five miles south of Madrid.

For nine months rioting flared up in Madrid. The mob sacked Esquilache's palace, and he and his wife barely escaped their vengeance. They even defied the hated (because foreign) Walloon Guard; pillaged the ammunition depots; closed the city gates; and virtually took over the capital.

Finally Charles III rescinded the order and dismissed Esquilache, who promptly went home to Italy. The Count of Aranda, who succeeded him, saved the face of the government by making the long cape and the big hat the official costume of the public executioner. The people, with more or less good humor, then consented to wear French styles, but maintained their independence by referring to this common European costume as "military dress." But the long cape did not wholly disappear for years.

By the time of the riots Goya had found work as an assistant in the workshop of Francisco Bayeu, to whom he was probably introduced by their former teacher, Luzán. Bayeu, twelve years older than Goya, was already a Court Painter; that is, he was one of several artists who had been recommended by their skill for a place on the royal payroll. In return, the Court Painters would execute works to decorate the walls and ceilings of the palaces, and paint portraits of the king and his family.

In a day long before photography, it was important for the royal family to be pictorially represented throughout their kingdom as well as abroad, for they were seldom seen in person by the public. Distributing these likenesses as widely as possible was good propaganda; they were given to foreign courts and embassies, and presented to the official buildings in provincial capitals. Needless to say, the portraits represented their subjects in a glamorous, not always truthful fashion, and always in gorgeous regal costumes. To supply this continual wide demand, a number of painters were employed and kept busy, and the royalty posed for them willingly as their duty to public information.

Francisco Bayeu (1734–95) was, next to Goya, the best Spanish painter of the eighteenth century, but there was a wide gap between their talents. An opportunist, Bayeu followed whatever style was in favor, and delivered what was wanted. Consequently, his work is so derivative

33

as to be barely distinguishable from that of his contemporaries. Generally speaking, it is formal, tight, and stiff, though well-designed and pleasingly colored. His religious and allegorical works tend to be melodramatic; his genre scenes to be spoiled by sentimental storytelling; his portraits forthright and heavy, with more emphasis on the details of elegant costume than on the character of the sitter. Federico de Madrazo, the celebrated nineteenth-century Spanish artist and connoisseur, said of Bayeu that he was "a fallen angel of art through the denial of his own personality and his submission to a style [neoclassicism] against which all his natural talents rebelled in vain."

Bayeu aimed to please the boss, and the boss was Anton Raphael Mengs (1728–79), First Court Painter, Director of the Royal Academy of Fine Arts of San Fernando, dictator of all official art in Spain. Mengs, whom Charles III had imported to fill this important position, was an eclectic even in his personal background. His father was Danish; he had been born in Bohemia (now largely Czechoslovakia); he had studied in Italy; he had found fame in Germany as the favorite painter of Frederick Augustus of Prussia.

In Rome, Mengs had met Johann Joachim Winckelmann (1717–68). By 1757 they had formulated the artistic principles of the neoclassic style. This was to sweep out the last litter of the decadent rococo style and install, as a sort of latter-day High Renaissance, the reworking of classical antiquity. It became the high style of the second half of the eighteenth century, known as the Age of Enlightenment or the Age of Reason.

Neoclassicism stemmed from the rediscovery of the ruins of Pompeii and Herculaneum. These revealed a way of life that had been simple, severe, and, to all appearances, serene—a calming contrast to the hectic vibrations of the restless, frilly, artificial rococo. What Winckelmann was to the scholarly development of this new aesthetic, Mengs was to its painting.

The trouble was that Mengs lacked the charisma that might have made him an evangelist of the new revelation. He could be only its devoted but uninspired professor. Winckelmann proclaimed that men could be great only insofar as they imitated the character of the ancient sages. Mengs declared that artists could be great only insofar as they imitated the works of ancient artists. There is a world of difference between the two points of view. When Mengs handed down his great commandment that art must be ruthlessly separated from reality and that beauty is not to be found in nature, he infected the aspiring souls of many young artists with an anemia from which they never recovered.

Not so with Goya. As a Spaniard he had an unquenchable devotion to truth and sincerity. As a peasant enveloped by the realism of nature, he loved and respected its purity and simplicity which taught unspoken, unformulated lessons heard by the private ear, seen with the inner eye. Toward the end of his long life, Goya wrote about:

> . . . professors full of mannerisms who always see lines and never form. But where do they find these lines in nature? . . . My eye never catches lines or details. I do not think of counting the hairs in the beard of the passerby, or the buttons on his coat. My brush cannot have better sight than its master. When these simple-minded teachers are face to face with nature, they are nearly always artificial and false. . . . They learn nothing from nature, the only true teacher of design.

35

Yet it was just such teachers—the influence of Mengs and his ape, the effeminate, Frenchified Bayeu—to whom Goya was subjected. Without conformity to their principles, recognition was impossible for a young painter in Spain. It is hardly likely that at the time he was first in Madrid Goya had formulated the philosophy just quoted, but even his earliest work shows that he saw and felt differently about art than his teachers.

Mengs's own work strikes the modern spectator as sentimental, artificial, and pretentious. He spent such an incredible amount of time perfecting minor points that his paintings are overwhelmed with detail. Their tight, narrow brushwork gives them a porcelain slickness that makes them seem more the product of a machine than of a thinking, feeling human being. Goya maintained that a picture was finished as soon as its effect is true. Mengs was more concerned with demonstrating his own technical perfection than with abstracting the truth of his subject. He was a master of getting himself between his subject and the spectator.

Mengs's influence dominated the Academy of San Fernando, of which he was director. In this capacity Mengs was trying to effect new rules for the government of the students and to alter the methods of instruction to conform to his own neoclassic principles. He had decreed that there are several aims in art: the sublime, the beautiful, the graceful, the expressive, the natural, the vitiated, and the easy. His Spanish colleagues had no use for such moralizing. They opposed Mengs's reforms and kept him from achieving all of them.

Their reasons were partly political. They were the king's men. However advanced a monarch Charles III may have been politically, he was not yet tired of the exhausted baroque style or of the artificiality of its effete

successor, the rococo. An aristocrat, he had only contempt
for the attitudes of the middle class, to whom his reforms
in trade were giving new power. The middle class believed
that wasteful frivolity should yield to the simplicity of
the neoclassic imitation of ancient austerity. Life was com-
plicated enough for Charles III for him to wish to add to its
difficulties by trying to achieve simplicity.

The reform party, however, favored the new style, just
as it favored giving the middle class of Spain greater advantages in order for the nation to be able to meet the competition of the more rapidly developing countries of Europe.
Art was not yet free. Goya, who was to do more to free it
from the tyranny of political patronage than any of his
contemporary artists, was caught, even before he was much
of an artist himself, between opposing political forces. The
dilemma confronted him again and again until finally he
solved it by trusting his own independence of spirit.

Mengs, nevertheless, increased the educational facilities
of the Academy. He procured for it plaster casts of the
statues which had been excavated at Herculaneum; he
persuaded Charles III to turn over to it the marbles and
bronzes Mengs had got for the king, and the classical
statues and busts Philip V had bought from the collection
of Queen Christina of Sweden; he got transferred to its
galleries the paintings confiscated from the houses of the
suppressed Order of Jesuits; he established a library.
Under his administration, classes in perspective were
opened on August 19, 1766; and the surgeon Augustin
Navarro was engaged to teach anatomy.

Confident in his own ability, and overconfident in the
training he had got in Zaragoza from Luzán and Ramirez,
Goya entered the annual competition for a scholarship
sponsored by the Academy soon after he had arrived in
Madrid. He got nowhere. The following year he again

won no prize. Possibly the judges considered Goya's work insufficiently disciplined in draughtsmanship, and its surfaces lacking the porcelain-like finish of the popular French style.

Goya may have consoled himself with watching Giovanni Battista Tiepolo (1696–1770) at work. Charles III had sent a ship to Venice to fetch this greatest of the rococo painters of Italy. Tiepolo executed some of his finest work on the ceilings of the new royal palace of the Spanish Bourbons, where he lavished his rich, warm Venetian colors, creating allegorical figures that float up and up beyond foamy pink clouds and into the blue sky until they seem part of heaven itself. Eventually the hostility of the king's confessor drove Tiepolo back to Italy. There, old and disappointed, he produced a series of prints that express the exact opposite of his celestial fantasies. These *Scherzi di Fantasia* satirize the vanities of this world. They may well have suggested to Goya his own mocking *Caprichos*.

Tiepolo's departure meant the triumph of Mengs, the favorite of the reform party, and the final victory of the cold, sentimental neoclassic style.

Tiepolo's son, Domenico (1727–1804), remained for awhile in Madrid. At that time his work was almost indistinguishable from his father's. It, too, made an impression on Goya. Goya probably felt close to the younger man, who was trying to free himself from parental influence just as Goya was struggling to emerge as an independent painter. Lorenzo, another son of the great Tiepolo, was also in Madrid; from him Goya may have learned the art of etching.

The three years and more that Goya spent as an apprentice galled him. Repressed by the strict discipline of Bayeu's studio, he escaped into a swaggering sort of life. According to legend he was a roistering bully, always ready for a fight or a girl, and was the dread of every aging husband who had a young wife. Probably this is an exaggeration. Goya was too prudent a peasant to dissipate on wild behavior the energies he was consecrating to painting, and too economical to fritter away his money on mere pleasures. Yet he was no anchorite.

As a country boy, he was dazzled by the delights and diversions of a big city. He believed that a painter should be stimulated by life itself. He loved the drama—there were two theaters in Madrid—and the intensity of actors. He adored bullfights. There were six a year in the Plaza Mayor. The enthusiasts were allowed to leap into the ring after the *toreros* had shown their skill. He improved his skill as a swordsman at the fencing arena in the Plaza Catalina, and was a popular favorite there with the spectators.

One of the sizable colony of Aragonese in the capital who stuck together and helped one another, Goya was the leader of the younger members. These supported the progressive policies of the Count of Aranda, the king's prime minister. Hence Goya found friends at Court among the strong Aragonese party there. The medieval atmosphere in Spain was at last fading, and fast. Democratic ideas of man and society were creeping in from France. There was a general feeling, half hopeful, half apprehensive, that the changes in process would eventually be revolutionary.

Goya tried again for a scholarship in the Academy competition of 1766. Each of the eight candidates was required to submit an oil painting six feet long by four and a half feet high. The subject assigned was: "Martha, wife of the Emperor Baldwin of Constantinople, asking King Alfonso the Wise, at Burgos, for a third of the ransom demanded for her husband by the Sultan of Egypt, and being granted the entire sum." Both theme and dimensions were typical. Still in provincial museums are acres of canvas covered with such tableaux of minor incidents in history. The aspirants worked for six months to execute their rendition of this pageantry.

Having reviewed the submissions, the jury met at eight-thirty in the morning of July 22. Among its nine members were Francisco Bayeu and Mariano Salvador Maëlla, each of whom would jointly become First Court Painter; Ventura Rodríguez, Spain's foremost architect; and Antonio and Alexander Gonzalez Velásquez, prominent painters—academicians all.

After greeting the competitors, the jury announced the subject for a second test of their skill. They would have two hours to execute it. The second theme was the dispute between Juan de Urbina and Diego de Paredes over which should possess the arms of the Marquis of Pescara, who had been defeated and killed by the Spanish army in Italy. The argument was to be depicted as taking place in the presence of that army in order for the candidates' ability with massed figures to be examined.

At eleven forty-five the jury inspected the results. They announced that, indeed, all submissions were worthy of a reward but that, alas, only three scholarships were available. The first went to Francisco Bayeu's twenty-year-old brother, Ramón, a painter much like Francisco himself. The name of the winner of the second is unknown. Gregorio Ferro, who never achieved much distinction thereafter, got the third. Goya's name was not even mentioned.

This third disappointment may have driven the young man, for relief of his despair, into the excesses that became part of the Goya legend. It is said that he was found one night lying in a street of the rough Lavapié section of Madrid with a dagger in his back. More likely he was advised by Bayeu to get rid of his provincialism by visiting Rome and studying its works of art, both ancient and Renaissance. Mengs was returning to Rome to refresh his inspiration at its source, and Bayeu himself was soon to go.

At any rate, Goya set out for the Eternal City, the goal of every young painter's dreams, toward the end of 1768. He went, as he later wrote in an official petition, at his own expense. Perhaps the money for the trip came from his father. Perhaps, as the legend has it, Goya earned his passage money by joining a *cuadrilla* and fighting bulls in the arenas between Madrid and the coast. In a gay letter Goya much later wrote to Zapater, he signed himself, "Francisco of the bullring," but he left no record of any extended experience as a matador.

After a rough voyage from the south of Spain, during which he was constantly seasick, Goya reached Rome in early 1769. The raw dampness of wintry Rome immediately brought him down with what was probably pneumonia. An old woman took him in and nursed him back to health in time for him to take part in the lascivious pre-Lenten carnivals and to witness the pomp of Pope Clement XIV's coronation.

He lived in the section of the city called Spanish because the Embassy of Spain was located there. Spaniards had no official location in Rome, as the French did at the Villa Medici. The area is still an artists' quarter—the region of the Piazza di Spagna nestled under the eastern slope of the Pincian Hill, on whose ridge sits twin-towered Santa Trinità dei Monti, from which cascade the marble Spanish steps. They were all there for Goya to gape at, and so, at the foot of the steps, was Pietro Bernini's curious fountain of the sunken boat, filled, as now, with the clear, sweet water of Rome.

Being under no obligation to patron or academy to justify his existence in Rome by producing work, Goya was a free-lancer. He is said to have supported himself by painting scenes of Spanish life, which sold quickly. If so, he was already taking his subject matter from the real life he knew and understood, not from the remote past, of which he had merely heard. Goya was then no intellectual; the noble sentiments of classical antiquity meant nothing to him. Even when, for some reason or other, he tackled a subject from classical mythology—a *Hercules and Omphale* and a *Cupid and Psyche* are the only two which survive—he missed the spirit of the original stories.

More probably he copied works to earn enough for his food. It is a reason why none of the paintings Goya did during this Roman episode have been definitely identified. Two, *Sacrifice to Vesta* and *Sacrifice to Pan*, which were exhibited in the Royal Academy Show, "Goya and His Times," in London, in 1963, may be Goya's work. They are Italianate and unsophisticated, and though they are signed and dated "1771," they are probably forgeries.

Goya seems to have had little to do with the other Spanish students of art in Rome who were connected with Preciado de la Vega's school there: Antonio de Ribera, Antonio Gonzalez Velásquez, Selma, Enguidanos, Carmona, and Villanueva. Probably he spent most of his time exploring the private collections of painting, to which Bayeu or Mengs could have got him introductions. In these he could study the quality of the old masters and draw his own conclusions from their principles of art.

Legends grew up around his stay in Rome. The Russian ambassador, Count Ivan Shuvalov, on the lookout for young painters to work for his Imperial mistress, Catherine the Great, is supposed to have invited him to Russia. It is an improbable story. Unless Shuvalov was unduly impressed by Goya's personality, which could be so pleasing as to get the young man into trouble, he could have found any number of more experienced artists. At any rate, Goya did not go to St. Petersburg.

He is said to have scaled the lantern of the dome of St. Peter's to carve his name above that of a French painter in order to prove that, as he supposedly said: "What a Frenchman can do, a Spaniard can do better." Some biographers say the building was the Tomb of Cecilia Metella, on the Appian Way; and they disagree as to whether the painter in question was Nicolas Poussin or Louis Michel Van Loo. It was, if either, probably the latter, for Van Loo, whom Philip V had imported to paint in Spain, was disliked there because he was a foreigner.

Rome was an unprincipled, disorderly city, full of intrigue political and romantic. Women, even of the best families, publicly displayed their often scantily concealed charms and invited further attentions from those who admired them. Goya may well have accepted. But there is no document to prove that he was jailed for trying to abduct a young nun from her convent. He was supposedly liberated from this serious charge, which could have meant death, only by the personal intervention of the Count of Viñaza, the Spanish ambassador, on the condition that Goya leave the city at once and forever.

What is known for certain is that he entered a competition for a prize offered by the Royal Academy of Fine Arts in Parma, the duchy from which came the next queen of Spain, Charles IV's infamous Maria Luisa. To demonstrate his eligibility, Goya sent from Rome to Count Rezzonico, the permanent secretary of the Academy, a painting illustrating Line 61 of the Sixth Book of Vergil's *Aeneid: Iam tandem Italiae fugientes prendimus oras* ("Now at last we grasp the elusive shores of Italy"). This was on April 20, 1771.

Self-portrait of Goya about the time he left Rome. *Collection of City Art Museum of St. Louis.*

At the end of May the theme for the competition was announced, a passage from a sonnet of Father Frugoni, the recently deceased permanent secretary of the Parmese academy: "Hannibal, from the summit of the Alps, casts his first glance over the land of Italy."

Probably Goya journeyed north to sample the artistic atmosphere of the Academy before he set to work executing the prescribed subject. He would have found it much the same as in Madrid, an imitation of both France and Spain, for the duchy had been handed over to the Spanish

Bourbons at the end of the War of the Austrian Succession in 1748. The influence of Mengs was strong there. One of his pupils was the official Court Painter of Don Felipe Bourbon and his wife, Louise Elizabeth, the daughter of Louis XIV of France. Goya found neoclassicism the favored style of the Academy.

He tried hard again to meet its demands. He failed. The jury of the Academy, which met on June 27, 1771, declared that: "If M. Goya in his composition had wandered less from the subject as outlined, and if he had put more truthfulness into his coloring, he would have swayed the votes for the first prize." Goya and the academicians had different notions of what truth is.

He did win the votes of six members of the jury with the following minority report: "In the second painting the Academy has remarked with pleasure a beautiful handling of the brush, a warmth of expression in Hannibal's eyes, and a quality of grandeur in the attitude of this general." Goya was cited as a "Roman, pupil of M. Vayeu [a misspelling of Bayeu], painter to the King of Spain."

The first prize went to Paolo Borroni, whom the world has long since forgotten; it can be seen in the museum of Parma. Goya's submissions have disappeared.

Goya's visit to Parma gave him a chance to see the frescoes of Correggio there in the convent of San Paolo and the cupola of the cathedral. The sensuous tone of these, their light effects, the color combinations, and the femininity of the angels in the cathedral dome Goya remembered when, nearly thirty years later, he was executing his own masterwork in frésco in San Antonio de la Florida, in Madrid.

Goya probably also visited Vicenza and Venice, for he seems to have seen the decorations of Tiepolo in the villas there. From these, as well as from the work Tiepolo did in

Madrid, Goya learned how to handle groups and movement. He also adopted Tiepolo's lighting and general plan of composition. But he never mastered Tiepolo's skill in foreshortening figures. As a result, Goya's ceiling decorations have none of the spectacular spaceward direction of the Venetian.

Another painter whose work he saw in Italy and who influenced him was Giuseppe Maria Crespi (1665–1747). Crespi's genre works are small in size, but they have an impressive monumentality. His style is reflected in Goya's paintings of washerwomen, water carriers, and other humble laborers; and his *Death of St. Joseph* and *The Last Communion of St. Joseph of Calasanza* are patterned after Crespi.

Still, insofar as practical results were concerned, Goya had accomplished little in Italy. The recognition he craved had eluded him as the Italian coast had fled from Aeneas' oars. Perhaps Mengs, who was also in Italy then, advised Goya to go back to Spain. Perhaps Goya himself, disappointed by his lack of success in a cosmopolitan society, decided to seek it in a less demanding environment. Perhaps he was simply homesick after a year and a half in a strange country.

At any rate, he went home, probably reaching Zaragoza in the late summer of 1771. He was not to leave Spain again for over sixty years.

3

On the Highway

St. James "the Greater" preached the gospel of Jesus Christ in Judea and Samaria for a few years after the Ascension and then went to Spain to sow the word of God. He is said by one authority to have made only one conversion there; another says that he gathered nine disciples, two of whom he left in Spain when he returned to Judea with the other seven. His departure was directed by the Virgin Mary, who appeared to him on the banks of the river Ebro and left her imprint on a pillar. This was said to have been in A.D. 40

Zaragoza's newly completely Cathedral of the Virgin of the Pillar marked the spot where the vision had appeared to the patron saint of Spain. A church had long stood there, but it had grown too small for the pilgrims who swarmed into Zaragoza to reverence the miraculous image and pray for its benefits. A huge new church had been planned by the painter Francisco Herrera in the churrigueresque style of the seventeenth century. This style, named for its leading practitioner, José Churriguera (1650–1723), represents baroque in the last stages of degeneracy; all the emphasis is on a highly decorated, picturesque effect. The church was finished according to the designs of Ventura Rodríguez, the most famous of Spanish eighteenth-century architects, in the rococo style.

The Committee on Art of the new cathedral had assigned the decoration of the dome above the sanctuary of the image to Antonio Gonzalez Velásquez. Velásquez painted the Virgin surrounded by angels in a style suited to the marble, bronze, silver, gold, and jewels of the shrine. He would have got the job of painting the choir also, but he asked too much money. The chairman of the Committee, Don Mathias Allué, began to shop around.

Zaragoza was not so large that his search remained a secret. Whether Goya, just home from Italy and like most newly returned travelers none too affluent, approached Don Mathias, or whether his old teacher Luzán or even Francisco Bayeu recommended Goya to the chairman, the two soon struck a bargain. Goya would do the work for 15,000 *reales* (about $1,000), which was forty per cent less than Velásquez had asked. Don Mathias agreed, providing the Academy of San Fernando approved the sketches which he required Goya to submit.

The terms and conditions would have humiliated a more experienced artist. Goya was in no position to cavil. He was twenty-six years old, half of his expected lifetime in those days of relatively early deaths, and he had achieved only a secondary distinction, and that in another country. Unless he had brought the picture of Hannibal with him, he had nothing much with which to demonstrate his ability, and he had never done any fresco painting.

An agreement was concluded on October 21, 1771. Goya got a copy of Palomino's treatise on painting, which had appeared in 1724, and followed its advice on fresco painting. Frescoing is no technique for a timid painter, but Goya was bold.

Three weeks later Goya submitted a sample of fresco painting to the Committee. They liked it, and directed him to prepare model sketches of the decorations he had in

The Adoration of the Name of the Lord, Goya's first fresco in the
Cathedral of El Pilar, Zaragoza.

mind. By November 11 he had submitted these. The Committee were so pleased that they waived the approval of the
Madrid Academy. Goya finished the work by the first of
the following July.

Its "superb tone and marvelous effect" pleased the Committee and the public. Goya warmed himself in the universal praise of his fellow citizens, for the effort had chilled
his fiery independence. To gain recognition he had bowed
to convention and given the Committee what they wanted,
not necessarily what he himself would have liked.

The subject is an allegory: *The Adoration of the Name
of the Lord*. Goya probably got the topic from some monk
or priest who appreciated its mystic overtones more than he

envisioned its pictorial possibilities. Goya had no compre-
hension of mysticism. Nor, apparently, did he recognize
that the subject lacked contrasts from which he could make
a dramatic composition. He leaped at the recommendation
just as he had at the commission.

By any but the most provincial standards, Goya's first
fresco in the Cathedral of El Pilar is not good. The only
thing that saves it from being offensive is its congruity with
the ornate, "busy" building itself. Approximately three
dozen figures—prophets, saints, angels, cherubim, and
seraphim—are stiffly disposed on and among all-too-solid
cloud banks, gazing more or less rapturously at a haloed
triangle in which are the Hebrew characters for Yahweh.
The "marvelous effect" is that of an insufficiently rehearsed
amateur pageant. All the uncomfortable-looking actors
seem to reflect Goya's possibly unconscious embarrassment
with a theme he imperfectly understood.

An artist is integrated only insofar as he can criticize his
own work, correct it when he finds it a crude or inaccurate
expression of his thinking, destroy it if it does not meet his
own standards. Goya had not yet reached this stage of pro-
fessionalism. Hungry for recognition, he accepted the
praise of inexperienced critics and decided to continue
painting what would be acceptable to them. The compro-
mise went against the grain in that he was thus being untrue to his own personality. He buried his disgruntlement
under his elation at his easy success. He was to learn that
dissatisfaction will not stay buried. The seeds of his later
discontent were planted on the ceiling of the choir of the
Cathedral of El Pilar.

He accepted other commissions as fast as they were
offered, for he had proved how rapidly he could work. The
monks of the Charterhouse of Aula Dei (Palace of God),
about five miles from Zaragoza, ordered eleven composi-

tions from him on the life of the Virgin and the infancy of Christ. The surfaces Goya had to cover were no less than fifteen feet wide, and some were thirty. In spite of Goya's speed—he worked this time in oil, not in true fresco —it took him two years to complete the assignment, though he covered one area of two hundred and fifty square yards in only forty days.

The monks let him alone, as the Committee of the cathedral had not done. But in his desire to please he continued to imitate. The murals for the Aula Dei reflect the Neapolitan rococo mannerism that Corrado Giaquinto (1703–65) had imported into Spain and made popular there. Also Goya tried out the lessons he had learned from Bayeu and Mengs. The result is more conventional painting, illuminated here and there with a touch of originality. These paintings are pictorially better than the El Pilar work, for at least the figures are dramatically lighted and set against dark backgrounds.

The murals were sadly damaged after the Charterhouse was sacked by the French during their attack on Zaragoza in 1808. Eight were ruined either by the elements or by bungling French restorers, Buffet and Amédée. The remainder, done in reds and yellows, are rather discordant in tone. *The Betrothal of the Virgin*, possibly the most attractive of them all, has natural figures, and there is a sincerely tender feeling in the gestures and expressions of Mary and Joseph.

Either simultaneously or immediately afterward, Goya was commissioned by the Aragonese nobility to paint seven religious decorations for the Sobradiel Palace in Zaragoza. His inspiration came from Italian engravings; indeed, these small compositions painted in oil are almost copies. The best of them, a *Descent from the Cross*, is plainly copied from the French painter Simon Vouet (1590–1649).

Four pictures Goya painted of saints for the parish church of Remolinos, about twenty miles north of Zaragoza, were in the style of the Aula Dei murals. So were the three he painted for the Church of Monte de Torrero. These perished in the War of Independence.

In this period Goya also executed his first surviving portrait, signed and dated 1774. It is of a local nobleman, Don Pedro Alcántara de Zúñiga, fourteenth Count of Miranda.

In the midst of all this energetic professional activity, Goya found time to woo Josefa, the daughter of Ramón Bayeu and Maria Subias, and the sister of Francisco and Ramón Bayeu. It is possible that Francisco promoted this romance between his promising pupil and his sister, for Josefa was older than Goya, perhaps by as much as ten years, and seemed to be withering on the vine. It is not unlikely either that Goya foresaw a certain advantage to him in being connected by marriage to so important a painter as Francisco Bayeu. They were married on July 25, 1773.

What Josefa was like is a matter of almost pure conjecture. A portrait Goya painted much later of a woman generally believed to be his wife shows her with reddish-gold hair, widely spaced, intelligent eyes, a rather stubborn mouth, a resigned air. Delicate, slender, and small, she was the type of woman Goya seemed to like best; he had small appreciation of the more voluptuous type of Spanish femininity. Doubtless Josefa was as uneducated as any other provincial Spanish girl, as unassuming and reticent. Living in the same household as her two painter brothers must have accustomed her to the vagaries of the artistic temperament, and she probably found herself able to put up with Goya's.

Certainly he never spoke ill of her. Instead, he let his "Pepa" accompany him on visits, when it was the custom for wives to stay at home. He took her to the seashore when she was ailing. In his letters to Martín Zapater he mentioned her frequently and quoted her remarks. His patrons and friends sent Josefa presents. For nearly forty years Francisco and Josefa Goya seem to have led a happy life together, marred only by the death of four of their five children. (There is no factual basis whatever for the persistent legend that Josefa bore twenty children.)

Goya decided to return to Madrid in the spring of 1775.

Josefa Goya. *Prado Museum, Madrid.*

PHOTO MAS, BARCELONA

More commissions could be procured there, and more important ones, than in Zaragoza. He was envious of the success of Francisco Bayeu, whose family he had recently joined, and was determined to surpass it as soon as he could complete his contracts in the provinces. Though he was confident of his ability to meet the challenge of Madrid, he took the precaution of getting promises of friendship and protection from the Fuentes family. He must have been aware that his work had been judged good by less than the top standards and that he needed the refinement of the capital. Possibly the overrefined and critical Bayeu had suggested this to him. Bayeu would take pains to see that his new brother-in-law did not detract in any way from his own position and reputation.

By September 6, 1775, Goya and Josefa were installed in Madrid in a house at No. 66, Carrera San Geronimo that belonged to the Marquesa of Campallano, one of the Fuentes. On that date and from that address Goya wrote his first letter to Martín Zapater, saying that he was painting a processional banner depicting St. Christopher on the one side and a *Mater Dolorosa* on the other. The whereabouts of this is unknown.

How domesticated Goya was after his return to the exciting capital would be hard to determine. On the one hand, his mind seems to have been on family matters and religion. Witness the banner he described to Zapater. A *Holy Family* also probably belongs to this period. It is touched with the sentimentality of Mengs, yet has a warm feeling of domesticity rarely found in the etherealized versions of the subject most Spanish painters produced. On the other hand, Goya probably could not resist the lure of the underworld he had loved before. Undoubtedly he spent a certain number of evenings in the company of its gypsies and dancers and bullfighters and swordsmen, while Josefa waited up for him alone.

They lived simply. The average Spaniard paid little attention to creature comforts. Furniture was plain and scanty, consisting of low chairs, low beds, and heavy tables. Bare painted walls were decorated, if at all, with religious engravings and religious figures. Floors were of tile covered with mats or perhaps only with straw and blankets. Heat was supplied by braziers, into which perfumed tablets could be thrown to kill the stench of stale cooking and humanity. Stew was the usual dish; wine was a luxury. If lower-class Spaniards chose to be extravagant, they squandered their money on clothes.

When the Bourbon dynasty had first come to Spain in 1700, the country lagged far behind the other nations of Europe. The basic reason was the Spanish reverence for tradition. The middle class believed that recovery would come about merely through intensifying measures that had served them well two hundred years before. Progress was anathema to them, and the Bourbons fought their resistance all the way.

To reinvigorate Spanish production, the Bourbons established factories for the manufacture of the goods for which Spain had once been famous. Among these were the glassworks at La Granja, and the porcelain factory in Buen Retiro. The most famous was the Royal Tapestry Manufactory of Santa Barbara, a suburb of Madrid, which Philip V had founded in 1720.

In line with Bourbon practice, Philip had imported a foreigner to direct it, a Fleming from Antwerp named Jacob van Goten. Van Goten naturally used the subject matter of his homeland and the designs of his compatriots. The principal ones were the Dutchman Philips Wouwerman (1619–68) and his brothers Pieter and Jan. They were all capable genre and landscape painters, but of a distant scene. Another favorite of van Goten's was David

Teniers the Younger (1610–90), the principal genre painter of the Flemish school of that time, famous for his scenes of peasant life in the manner of his in-laws, the Brueghels.

Both Wouwerman and Teniers were highly regarded by eighteenth-century collectors, who thought them more refined than their earthy masters, Pieter Brueghel the Elder and Hieronymus Bosch. Other foreign designers for the tapestry works were the Italians Provaccini, Giordano, and Lorenzo Tiepolo, and the Frenchman René Antoine Houasse.

By the time van Goten's son, Cornelius, had succeeded him as manager of the tapestry factory, the output had become conventionalized, mechanical, and stale. The subjects were mythological and allegorical, and were being executed in a second-rate style.

In 1762, Charles III, on the recommendation of his minister, the progressive José Moniño, later Count of Floridablanca, made Mengs his adviser on the revival of the industry. Recognizing that the Flemish genre scenes had been the best of the factory's output in the past, Mengs decided that future subjects were to be the everyday life of contemporary Spain. To execute them he engaged only Spanish painters: Francisco and Ramón Bayeu, Andrea de Calleja, José del Castillo, Mariano Salvador Maëlla, Manuel Napoli, and Antonio Gonzalez Velásquez.

On the recommendation of Francisco Bayeu, who was making an effort to look out for his sister and her unpredictable husband, and at the same time butter his own bread, Goya's name was submitted to Mengs as a possible designer of tapestry cartoons. Mengs was always in need of recruits for his stable of cartoonists, for the work distracted painters from their more personal efforts. Mengs asked Goya to submit a subject.

The general theme pleased Goya. At last he could interpret something he understood, not some abstraction from religious lore or some obscure incident from remote history. There could be physical action, not the posing of waxwork tableaux. If he still had to bow to the popular taste, at least he could bring to that purely decorative style some elements of reality.

Bayeu left Goya to his own devices. Goya chose for his first cartoon—that is, a painting designed to be reproduced in some other medium—a wild-boar hunt. It was a topic he thought would appeal to the hunt-loving King Charles III, and one that Goya himself relished for the adventure implicit in it. He, too, was an enthusiastic hunter. He delivered the painting on May 24, 1775, and was paid the equivalent of about $375 for it. On the following June 18, he was awarded a commission for more tapestry cartoons.

From then on, until 1780, the forty more he painted occupied the major part of his time. All of them were destined, in woven form, for the refurbishing of rooms that had grown shabby in the royal palaces: ten for the dining room of the royal children, finished by January, 1778; seven more by April 27, 1778, for the bedroom of the princess of the Asturias, the wife of the crown prince; seven more by January 5, 1779, for her husband's bedroom; and the rest, completed by January 27, 1780, for various other chambers. This achievement is all the more heroic in that Goya was seriously ill in April, 1777, and the previous January had seen his first child, Vicente Anastasio, be born and die. He was living then at No. 1, Calle Espejo.

The tapestries, all of which deal with phases of the national life of Spain, brought Goya recognition. By 1778 Antonio Ponz would refer to him in his *Viaje de España* as "professor of painting" and comment on his ability. (By "professor" Ponz meant not a teacher but a well-known practitioner.)

The cartoons also identified Goya with the optimistic

reform party, which emphasized nationalism as opposed to the imitation of French and other foreign manners. It was becoming stylish in certain quarters to appreciate the everyday things. The plays of Ramón de la Cruz (1731-94), for example, were treating the lower classes seriously and were serving to revitalize the Spanish theater.

The connection was not wholly a professional one; Goya's convictions entered into it. His sympathy with the common people, to which class he belonged, led him almost to idealize them. He wanted to make a distinction, by means of costume, gestures, and facial types, between the ingredients of human society and its fortuitous, artificial classes. To him the people were not amusing, as they were to the aristocracy. He saw them working and playing and suffering as human beings. Titles and fortunes meant nothing in comparison with this reality. Here was the truth of nature and of human life.

A few of Goya's tapestry cartoons, like *The Crockery Vendor*, contain a slight touch of satire; the rest have no object but mindless decoration. Their bright colors are those of the dye vat, not of nature; they are charming, but they produce no other emotional response, or any intellectual one.

The action in them is mannered. They are Spanish versions of French "pastoral" scenes, in which dainty, sophisticated people are playing at being crude rustics. The *majos* and the *majas* in them wear their traditional costumes, but their clothes are too brand new to be realistic, for one thing. They are not the bold, arrogant characters they would become in Goya's later, more independent work.

Typical is *Confidences in a Park,* in the Museum of Fine Arts, Houston, Texas. Here a *maja* and two *majos* are artificially posed against a leafy background. They are in splendid national costume, but they are hardly the types Goya saw daily.

Confidences in a Park, one of Goya's early tapestry cartoons. *Museum of Fine Arts, Houston, Samuel H. Kress Collection.*

This one could have brought the charge from the discomfited Cornelius van Goten that Goya had no respect for the technique of tapestry. Van Goten complained to the palace that Goya sent in "dandies and girls with so much decoration of coifs, fal-lals, gauzes, etc., that much time is wasted on them and the work is unproductive."

Goya corrected his style, but probably only after fuming at such interference.

The tapestries themselves, most of which are in the Escorial Palace, fifteen miles north of Madrid, show that he came to understand the purpose to which his paintings would be put. The cartoons were forgotten for nearly a century. In 1869 they were found rolled up in a palace storeroom. Most of them now hang in galleries of their own in the Prado Museum.

The earliest of this first series of tapestry cartoons are the work of a clumsy, provincial painter more eager to please than to express any significant originality. There are many borrowings in them: from the spirited genre scenes of the Venetian Guardi family and of Pietro Longhi; from the landscapes of the French painters Boucher and Fragonard; from Goya's Frenchified Spanish contemporary, Luis Paret y Alcazar.

As he worked at the series, however, Goya increased his skill. He abandoned "overall" compositions—canvases entirely filled with figures, like the *Picnic on the Banks of the Manzanares*, sometimes thought to be the first of the series —in favor of cleanly outlined single figures or groups. (He would never master the organization of many different elements or details.) By 1778 he had learned to place shadowed forms against a strongly lighted background without losing the values of the planes. This arrangement became a prominent characteristic of Goya's style; it grew more and more simplified as he matured.

In spite of their flaws, the cartoons are much more distinguished than the output of Goya's fellow designers. Goya's have humor and a loving understanding of the subject. His figures live and move. Even when they are artificially posed, they have a stylish flair. Goya's colors are contrasted so as to make his scenes, all of which have plenty of action, fairly vibrate with animation. The work of the other cartoonists is static and dull in comparison.

In 1778, while Goya was at work on this series, Charles III decided that the paintings in the royal collection, locked away from the public in the ten different royal residences, should be brought together in Madrid and made known to the world. Doubtless the reform party got Mengs to suggest this move as part of its intention to reestablish Spain in the community of civilized nations. Charles III himself was no connoisseur. Mengs had to persuade him not to destroy the magnificent nudes of Titian and Rubens, which the king thought immoral and irreligious. By a decree of the Council of Trent in 1563, the nude in painting and sculpture was to be sanctioned thereafter only in mythological subjects.

The only way in which this circulation of the paintings could be accomplished was to have them copied as engravings. Artists were assigned to this laborious, uncreative task, Goya among them.

The job was not without its compensations. At last there could be revealed to the provincial Spanish painters the treasures the Hapsburg dynasty had assembled from the distant reaches of their empire. For the first time they set eyes on the long-hidden masterpieces of Dürer and Brueghel and Bosch, of Raphael and Titian and Rubens, Murillo and Velázquez.

Velázquez had been almost forgotten in Spain, and his canvases were not the most admired of the collection.

Mengs grudgingly and rather patronizingly gave Velázquez his due, and decided that certain of the works of this
Spanish national genius should be engraved. They were
assigned to Goya, possibly because he was the newcomer
to Mengs's stable of artists.

In Velázquez, Goya found a kindred spirit who had expressed in superb fashion the Spain he knew and loved.
Velázquez' work is rather lacking in invention and originality; but his handling of light and form and space, his
color, and his sense of style have never been surpassed.
Among his gifts is a fine irony that appealed to Goya's
own humor. Both artists perceived the gap in human nature between the ideal and the actual, and exposed the
pretensions of those who mistook their identity.

From copying Velázquez' portraits Goya learned how to
abstract out of a face the essentials which express the
individuality of a sitter, however commonplace his features.
The subjects thus became spiritualized. He learned, too,
how Velázquez could make a pose, a gesture, even a background express a subject's psychology. Being compelled to
translate Velázquez' colors into the black and white of an
engraving, Goya began to understand the values of pig-
ments. No longer would he produce the clashing reds and
yellows which make his Aula Dei murals crude. He also
learned from the master how to unify light and atmosphere
and avoid the melodramatic contrasts of his Zaragoza work.
From this experience onward, Goya's own methods became more and more subtle.

Goya had probably learned etching from the 1691 text-
book of José Garcia Hidalgo, Court Painter to Philip V.
Before he tackled the Velázquez assignment he had made
only three etchings: *The Flight into Egypt, San Francisco
de Paula,* and *San Isidro el Labrador.* The drawing of the
first is poor; the second shows some of the light effects that

later would make Goya's engravings superlative; the third is unfinished. Goya was not yet sufficiently experienced in abstracting the essence of his subject by leaving out individualizing particulars to be completely successful in a medium that demands the utmost economy.

Furthermore, Goya was not cut out to be a copyist. He could not keep his own personality out of the Velázquezs he was reproducing. The result is that the series of eighteen etchings has some of both artists in them, but not enough of either to make them eloquent. Of them all, Goya's versions of Velázquez' *Aesop* and his *Menippus* come off best. Probably Goya sympathized with Velázquez' treatment of the two ancients, whom he interpreted as contemporary old Spanish beggars. This was a realism Goya liked.

The next year, 1779, Goya made an independent etching—*The Garroted Man*. It is his finest print before the *Caprichos* of 1796–98. Here first appears the theme of death and suffering which figures largely in Goya's later work. Detail is subordinated, as it should be in a black-and-white etching, to an effect of light. By this time Goya had not only studied Velázquez, he had digested him.

Later Goya said that his three masters were nature (by which he meant reality), Velàzquez, and Rembrandt. He had not yet studied the great Dutchman, and it is unlikely that he ever saw many of Rembrandt's paintings. The Academy, however, owned engravings of them that Goya could have examined. It was Rembrandt's etchings that later had the greatest influence on him.

The tapestry cartoons and the series of Velázquez etchings pleased the Court sufficiently for Goya to be presented to the royal family on January 9, 1779. For the peasant from tiny Fuendetodos, this was a mighty occasion. He could not wait to tell Martín Zapater how he had risen in the professional and now the social scale. He knew that loyal Martín would spread the news among the home folks. The very same day that he was introduced into the palace he wrote: "I was honored by the king, the prince, and princess [the future Charles IV and his wife Maria Luisa], to whom, by the grace of God, I was able to show four pictures. I kissed their hands, a good fortune that until then I had never had. As to their liking my work, I assure you I could not have wished for more."

In the same letter Goya adds: "the rough draft you have is the invention of Francisco [Bayeu], but the execution is mine." He was referring to a *Crucifixion* he was preparing to submit as a candidate for membership in the Academy of San Fernando. It is indeed an academic work. There is nothing in the body of Christ to suggest agony; in fact, the rather soft figure is comfortably posed on a small platform that Goya invented out of a common-sense deduction that the feet of Christ could hardly have been attached to the upright beam of the cross. Only the nails through the feet—or, rather, the nailheads placed on the insteps—would keep the figure from moving away if it wished to do so.

The composition therefore lacks the intensity other painters have given the supreme drama of the Christian faith. The expression on Christ's face suggests hysterical anguish; otherwise Goya seems to have assumed, in spite of the explicitness of the Gospels on the point, that Christ's divinity sublimated His physical suffering. Furthermore, the cross is isolated from the elements, which the Evangelists say were in commotion, and from any of the traditional mourning followers who could help stimulate the emotions of the spectator.

Goya was not one to let his presentation at Court go without being followed up. On July 24, 1779, he submitted a petition to be made a Court Painter. He stressed

64

his work in Zaragoza, and his experience in Rome at his own expense, and gave Mengs as a reference. The petition was turned down on the grounds that Goya was not yet well enough known for such a distinction to be granted.

Possibly the puritanical Charles III had heard and disapproved of Goya's supposedly wild life. The gossip could have reached the king through rivals envious of Goya, and they may have conspired to keep Goya from the honor he sought. He had acquired enemies who had no wish to see his talents—if nothing else, he was a much faster worker than they—surpass their own. He wrote Zapater: "Nothing

Crucifixion. *Prado Museum, Madrid.*
PHOTO MAS, BARCELONA

is going to rid me of the notion from now on that my enemies will be more numerous and more violent." Already
Goya was suffering from delusions of persecution.

After this disappointment, which Goya took with poor
grace, he had to be content with membership in the Royal
Academy of Fine Arts of San Fernando. He submitted his
Crucifixion with his application on July 5, 1780. Two days
later he was unanimously elected.

4

A Prophet in his Own Country

Election to the Academy of San Fernando was by no means
all that Goya thought he deserved. The other members
were men to whom he had shown himself superior, or from
whose influence he was struggling to break away. The stubborn fact that without their approval and support he would
get even less recognition was bitter to him. His very admis-
sion to the powerful clique of academicians had been pred-
icated on his willingness to paint not necessarily so well as
they, but simply in their manner. They had passed favor-
ably on his *Crucifixion,* but probably not without a suspi-
cious glance at its vigorous brushwork, which indicated a
rebellious individualism lurking under Goya's submissive-
ness.

Goya's rejection by the Court kept him still out of the
influential society of Madrid. He felt himself isolated. The
only outlet for his bruised feelings were the long letters he
wrote to Martín Zapater. The more he believed himself
persecuted by his enemies, the more he acknowledged to
himself that they would not be harassing him if they were
not afraid his genius would displace them. He began retreating into himself. In his mind he transformed the envy,
the sham, the pretentiousness of the world he wanted into
monsters crouching in ambush to spring upon him. The
critical *Crucifixion* assumed an ironic personal meaning.
He looked at the world in terms of his own personality.

Fate he saw against him in other ways as well. Josefa had produced another child, on October 9, 1779, a daughter they named Maria del Pilar Dionisia. They were living then at No. 1, Calle del Desengaño. Now the little girl was dead. The home Goya longed to see bright and noisy with children was still gloomy and silent. Another child was on the way, but he could easily imagine that it would not be with them long. Everything was conspiring to keep him from all he wanted most.

In this dark mood Goya prepared to return to Zaragoza. The Committee on Art of the Cathedral of El Pilar had found enough money for the work of completing the decorations to continue. They approached their famous native son, Francisco Bayeu, who did not consent to do the work —he was too engaged in more important projects in the metropolis—but agreed to superintend it. The actual painters would be his brother-in-law Goya and his own brother, Ramón.

To Goya the assignment was just another hand-me-down commission. In addition, it would have to be done in a manner to please Bayeu and the indecisive Committee, who knew nothing about art but definitely knew what they wanted and what they would pay for. It was also a commission for more religious subjects. Goya's inspiration would have to come from sources other than his imagination.

There was nothing he could do but accept. For him to refuse would be to antagonize his influential brother-in-law. On May 10, 1780, he wrote to Zapater that he was coming back to Zaragoza, and would Martín please see to getting him a house and some furnishings. "I don't want much in the way of possessions," Goya wrote. "With a print of Our Lady of the Pillar, a table, five chairs, a skillet, a guitar, a checkerboard, and a lamp, anything else would be superfluous."

He tried to rationalize returning to a simple, uncompetitive life. "Air and freedom and a fine life," he had written Zapater, "that's my credo." His physical needs certainly were few. His spiritual ones would be met by a childish trust in the protection of a religious picture. Music and a game would relax nerves stretched taut by a day at the easel.

The summer dragged on in Madrid. Josefa was pregnant. The long, jolting, two-hundred-mile journey to Zaragoza would be impossible for her. They were bored. "Josefa," Goya wrote Zapater on August 9, "wants me to tell you that the home is woman's grave. She thinks the place sad." Then, on August 22, the baby made its appearance, a second son they named Francisco de Paula Antonio Benito. "Thank God, a very healthy boy," the father wrote, unaware that the child would not live. "Now we will come sooner than I thought."

When the little family finally did arrive in Zaragoza, Goya found the atmosphere around the cathedral strained because of his delay. He did not have his sketches ready for another month. Not until October 5 were they approved. The Committee praised them.

Goya went to work on the first assignment without having made any full-scale cartoons. He had apparently decided to trust to the inspiration of the moment as he stood on the scaffolding under the dome of one of the church's many cupolas. When Francisco Bayeu arrived in December, he was shocked at this omission, quite contrary to accepted procedures. To the academically minded Bayeu, Goya was flouting authority—his. He accused Goya of irresponsibility.

But Goya was now himself a member of the Academy. Furthermore, the Committee had previously—in April, 1774—approached him directly to decorate two domes and four cupolas, and he had then, before going to Madrid, completed a *Coronation of the Virgin,* which pleased them. Determined not to take his officious brother-in-law's opinions so agreeably as before, Goya reminded Bayeu of all this.

Bayeu was astonished to find Goya so stubborn, and was perturbed at the speed with which he was working. Probably Goya's irritation had made him paint more feverishly than ever. In three months he completed his huge fresco of *The Virgin, Queen of the Martyrs.*

There is nothing in this vast expanse of clouds, peopled with holy figures, to distinguish it from dozens of other contemporary church paintings. The technique is more professional than in Goya's earlier work in the cathedral, but the treatment is equally banal. Still, Goya had delivered just what had been asked for.

In February, 1781, Bayeu climbed up on the scaffolding to inspect the fresco, and began to find fault with it. Goya exploded.

"Are people birds," he shouted at Bayeu, "that they will see it from up here? Go down and look at it. It is meant to be seen from the floor."

Bayeu leaned over the scaffolding and pointed to a ragged beggar in the church. He told Goya to observe the picturesque effect of the figure when seen from above.

"If that beggar," said Bayeu, "looks well close to and at a distance, your painting should also."

Goya was quick to see that the criticism had little validity. Stormily he rejected it. He demonstrated that he had followed Bayeu's instructions and example. He had done so, in fact, to such a degree that in criticizing the fresco Bayeu was really condemning his own principles.

Such apparently was the case. Bayeu was not so displeased with the work as he was with Goya's independence. As Goya himself later pointed out, Bayeu was angry because his former pupil was not showing the respect due his teacher.

Bayeu reported to the Committee that he could no longer take responsibility for the work Goya was executing on the cathedral ceilings. Then with fiendish cunning he added that he believed that Goya should continue in his own way.

The Committee reacted just as Bayeu knew they would. They began to imagine flaws in Goya's work. To compound their stupidity they called in the public. These good people, even more unqualified to judge and utterly unable to invent opinions of their own, naturally saw defects they had been practically told to see.

Their untutored eyes focused on the allegorical figure of Charity which Goya had painted on one of the four pendentives (inverted triangles of masonry supporting the dome) of the cupola. There were to be three others—Faith, Fortitude, and Patience—sketches for which Goya had submitted on March 10. These are the only portions of the work as a whole in which Goya showed any originality at all.

Desperately searching for something to criticize, as Bayeu had hinted they should, the public decided that the quite feminine form representing Charity was insufficiently draped. It was, they said, indecent.

The Committee asked Goya to correct his work. He should, they added, also make it conform more to the style of his co-worker, the uninspired Ramón Bayeu. Their report emphasized "the fact that Goya had come to paint owing, in large measure, to the influence and praise of his brother-in-law," to whom he should be more subservient.

The same Mathias Allué who had given Goya his first commission nearly ten years before was appointed to "supervise the artist and his work and to make such criticisms as he thought might be necessary. He should also

71

make it clear to Goya how grateful he should be to Don Francisco Bayeu for appointing him to be his assistant."

Goya's blood boiled. It was bad enough to have to take Bayeu's supervision, but to have to follow that of a man illiterate in art was worse than humiliating, it was insulting. He refused to change his work or have it altered, as had been suggested, by some "dauber chosen at random." The "dauber" was obviously to be Bayeu himself.

By this time the quarrel was all over town. Everyone knew that Goya had been forbidden to finish the figures on the pendentives without Bayeu's express approval. Bayeu must be right; after all, he was older, and he was a Court Painter. His fellow citizens began to remember that Goya had always been wild and stubborn.

In reply to the Committee, Goya drew up the longest piece of writing to survive from his hand, and the best expressed. The calm Martín Zapater may have suggested it to him as a proceeding more proper than raging at the Committee or getting into fights with his neighbors. Probably Zapater helped Goya write it, for the style of the document is more formal and polished than that of Goya's naïve letters.

It was his protest against "the strange and violent hostility," the "torrent of provocations injurious to his honor and reputation," the "calumnies against him"—all of which stemmed from the "hypocritical" Don Francisco Bayeu, who "feared the success of the signer of these lines, a success already obtained at the Court" and who had tried to discredit Goya because he "coveted the order for himself."

The last thrust was probably untrue. Goya was too furious to be entirely just. He was rebelling against the implication that he was only a hireling, subject to every dictate of his masters, not a free artist, not even a free soul.

Goya emphasized that he had undertaken the entire job

"on the understanding that he should do one of the parts by himself . . . considering that the fact that he was an honored member of the Academy of San Fernando . . . would not allow him to submit to another painter without damage to his own reputation."

Against the obdurate, insensitive Committee, Goya then raised the immemorial cry of the creative spirit. "The honor of an artist," he wrote, "is a delicate thing. All his reputation and his fortune depend on it. If it is darkened even by a shadow, the very means by which an artist lives is destroyed. An artist must defend himself as well as he can. If he did not, even feebly, he would lose the greatest gift God has given him."

Then Goya proposed a settlement of the whole vicious quarrel. If the work could be judged by an impartial expert in matters of art, he would abide by that man's decision. He offered to bring to Zaragoza at his own expense one of his fellow members in the Academy—Mariano Salvador Maëlla or Antonio Gonzalez Velásquez. He sent the letter off to the Committee on March 17.

Now the Committee was in trouble. If Goya packed up and quit, as he threatened to do, his unfinished work would have to be reassigned. Time and money would have been wasted. The Committee were practical men, if nothing else.

Mathias Allué had a happy thought. He approached Father Felix Salzedo, a monk of the Charterhouse of Aula Dei, who was a trusted friend of Goya and may even have started him on his artistic career. Would Father Salzedo try to soothe his volcanic protégé?

On March 30, the monk wrote Goya a little sermon on humility. "There is nothing nobler," he preached, "nothing more Christian and truly pious, than for a man of action to humble himself before another man, according to reason and the will of God. To lower one's pride is always heroic and meritorious."

Then he took a more practical approach. "Why get involved in a matter of form with the Committee," he asked, "when they may be very useful to you and your family? This is the first important job you have had. It would be a pity if you were to let it end in a lawsuit. Even if you won, you would get a reputation for being stubborn and vain. If you go on behaving like this, you will make your brother-in-law your enemy for life, and cause a public scandal. Think it over slowly."

Goya did. Slowly his peasant prudence—perhaps with Zapater's help—overruled his artist's passion. Unwillingly he admitted to himself that Francisco Bayeu's hostility could wreck him in Madrid, where he was not actually so well established as he would like to believe. He began to be afraid of what Bayeu could do to him. Another lurking monster joined the swarm in his mind.

A week later, on April 6, Goya replied to his "bosom friend" Father Salzedo that he would redesign the pendentives and submit sketches for Bayeu's approval.

Smoldering with resentment, Goya finished the work he had started. In May, on the same day he completed it, he went to the Committee and demanded his pay—what he later called "the silver of my shame." But his suppressed rage burst out and he refused to risk his reputation by doing any more work for the Committee. He also renewed his personal feud with Francisco Bayeu.

The Committee had had enough. They took Goya at his word and wrote him that in no circumstances would he be permitted to do any further work in their cathedral. Maliciously they added that their chairman, Mathias Allué, would present a gold medal to Josefa Goya in recognition of the skillful assistance her brother had given in the decoration of the church. As Francisco Bayeu's sister, they said, she fully deserved this honor.

Josefa accepted the token, though she must have known it was a final humiliation to her husband, who got nothing. Perhaps she thought his rebelliousness needed this rebuke. Undoubtedly she shared her brother's views on art. But she had little chance to display the medal in Zaragoza. Goya quit the town like St. Theresa leaving Avila. The family were back in Madrid before the end of June.

Ramón Bayeu was given the order for the other dome Goya was to have frescoed.

For years this poisonous quarrel rankled in Goya's mind and infected his thoughts. "At the mere thought of Zaragoza," he wrote Zapater, "and those paintings, my blood seethes. . . . Don't remind me of it," he added. "It has given me too much cause for grief. I am amused by your anxiety over my affairs, but I don't want to hear any more about the business."

The sense of having been unjustly treated affected Goya's health. He grew nervous and irritable. Morbidly he believed in a cabal bent on destroying him. His ambition and his complete belief in his abilities and his capabilities made him interpret his lack of acceptance by more mature painters and by the public as hostility. Actually it was only indifference.

It was nearly ten years before he patched things up with Francisco Bayeu, and even longer before Goya could write Zapater that the fears he had had of Bayeu's ruining his career "made him laugh a lot."

If, indeed, Francisco Bayeu would have been so vindictive, he was powerless to obstruct Goya's first opportunity to vindicate the reputation that had been besmirched in Zaragoza. Goya's dashed hopes rebounded almost as soon as he was back in the capital.

On July 25, 1781, he wrote to Zapater exuberantly, and not without exaggeration, that "the Court has done me the honor of choosing me as one to be entrusted with an order." It was a commission to paint an altarpiece for one of the seven minor altars of the brand-new Church of San Francisco el Grande in Madrid.

This church, designed by Ventura Rodríguez, was the latest showplace of the capital Charles III was still bent on beautifying. Unfortunately, it is not one of the city's best buildings. Its magnificence is chilled by the severity of its neoclassic design—a rotunda striped with marble pilasters beneath a 108-foot dome. But the aging king, now deeply concerned with the salvation of his soul, adored it. He announced a competition, the entries to be decorations for the church, and gave commissions to all the prominent painters, Francisco Bayeu among them. Bayeu, in fact, was entrusted with the high altar itself. The results of the contest would determine who was the best painter in Spain.

It was hardly Bayeu who recommended Goya to Charles III. It may have been Ventura Rodríguez, the State Architect of the City of Madrid, a close friend of Goya. Goya painted a portrait of him in 1784 at the order of the wife of the Infante Don Luis, brother of Charles III. Rodríguez had designed the infante's palace of Boadilla. The architect probably used his influence in Goya's behalf with the Count of Floridablanca, the prime minister.

Still overestimating his abilities, Goya was certain of a triumph. "I was very much crushed," he wrote Zapater, referring to his humiliation in Zaragoza, "but it has pleased God to comfort me."

What would comfort him more, Goya clearly implied, was for Zapater to spread the news around Zaragoza where it would do the most good. He even sent Zapater the invitation to the competition, signed by Floridablanca, in order that loyal Martín could "confound those vile slanderers who doubted my value."

Throughout August and September, 1781, Goya worked hard on cartoons for the altarpiece. It was to be 9 yards high by 4½ wide. Goya's letters to Zapater keep referring to his progress, intimating how much the commission meant to him and how eager he was to produce a master-piece. At least four of these preliminary studies remain. It was two years before Goya finished it.

The months meanwhile were not smooth ones. The con-flict in Zaragoza had been either the cause or the result of a nervous disorder that bothered Goya. Probably it emanated physiologically from some aural maladjustment. It made Goya grow egocentric, brusque, and fiercely re-sentful of criticism. At the same time he was becoming a savage critic himself.

A writer who had presumed to disparage Goya's work once found the painter's hat suddenly jammed down over his face, and heard: "From now on, you have respect for a head big enough to wear this hat."

Another critic got a brush full of paint snapped in his face. "Tit for tat," Goya explained. "You disfigure me in your books; I'll disfigure you in my studio."

On December 17, 1781, Goya's father died in Zaragoza and was buried in the principal nave of the little Church of San Miguel de los Navarros. He left no will because, as he had said, he had nothing to leave.

Goya took the loss hard. He had known at least a month beforehand that the old man was in his last illness, but had been unable to visit him. He himself felt his own end might be near. "We who have been such rascals," he wrote Zapater, "need to mend our ways in the little time we have left."

Then, on April 13, 1782, Josefa gave birth to a daughter,

who apparently did not live long enough to be given a
name. And the following November, Goya's sister Rita
died suddenly.

These deaths gravely affected Goya. "I am without
strength, and cannot work much," he wrote Zapater. "Pray
to the Virgin to give me more desire to work."

The picture for San Francisco el Grande was forcing
him into a crisis of the conflict between the necessity of his
being sincere in a religious painting and his lack of true
religious feeling. To release his tensions he went hunting
frequently. He wished he could go back to Zaragoza and
"take nothing from no one" and go hunting with his dear
Martín every single day.

What partially revived his spirits was a wider acquaintance with the grandees of the Court. Ventura Rodríguez
had apparently introduced him to several of them, and by
January 22, 1783, he had got the coveted commission of
painting a portrait of the highly influential prime minister.

Don José Moniño y Redondo, created Count of Floridablanca later in 1783, was fifty-five years old at the time. He
had been an important member of the king's legal council
before becoming prime minister in 1777. From then until
1792 his career was one of the most brilliant and successful
in Spanish history. He was a clean-living, dedicated man,
who gave an initial impression of being gloomy and intro-
spective. But he had polished manners, was considerate of
others, and could be cordial.

How well Goya knew him is doubtful, but the count's
wife certainly knew and liked the painter—the first of
many women of the Court who were to find his company
pleasing. He wrote to Zapater that he had been with her
"for two hours after her dinner."

It is hard to determine what Goya's charm consisted of.
In spite of his rugged muscularity, he was hardly good-

looking. His peasant simplicity makes the assumption absurd that he could or would converse in the elegantly brittle style of the *petimetres*—the dandies of the day—or that he would dress in their extreme fashions. Perhaps it was his adaptations of the ways of the lower classes that made him popular, for the Court ladies were adopting bullfighters and were beginning to dress and pose as *majas*. Or it may have been a part of the general French influence on the Court. Jean-Jacques Rousseau had made the simple, natural man an enviable character in France, where the unaffected Benjamin Franklin would be a darling of society.

The portrait of Floridablanca went slowly. Portraiture was not wholly a new field for Goya, but he did not yet feel at home in it. Nor had he by any means developed the individual style that was to make him one of the world's greatest portraitists. Recognizing the prestige value of the commission, Goya worked earnestly at it. Floridablanca gave him only one sitting, on April 26—for the head—but Goya got a likeness that he wrote Zapater was good.

How truly like the prime minister it was is doubtful. Goya was probably too prudent to probe deeply into the man's character, which was far from forthright. Goya did, however, capture the minister's single-mindedness in the wide-spaced, tense eyes, staring as if to let nothing escape them, and in the narrow face they dominated.

The rest of the canvas is mediocre, breathing a stiff and shallow formality that makes it scarcely distinguishable from any other "official" portrait of the time. Its worst flaw is that it is fearfully cluttered. Goya included not only the minister, unfortunately in almost the dead center of the picture, but also the count's secretary, a portrait of Charles III on the wall, and the painter himself. Goya is holding a frame for Floridablanca to inspect, but the minister is singu-

The Count of Floridablanca. *Collection of the Marqués de Valdueza, Madrid.*

80

larly uninterested in it. There is unconscious humor in Goya's humble posing of himself and in the way he has shortened his own stature to make the short count seem taller. An ornate clock on a table, books, maps, charts, and letters litter the rest of the space. By some miracle of refraction the light, which comes from behind the figures, floods their fronts.

Goya reported to Zapater that Floridablanca was "very well satisfied" with the portrait when finally it was done, over six months after Goya had begun it. If he expected anything more from the minister, however, he was disappointed. Dismissing him as he might have sent away any tradesman with whose services he was content, Floridablanca merely said: "We shall meet later."

Three months later there had been no meeting. "Everyone is astonished," Goya wrote his friend, "that nothing should have come from the Minister of State after the portrait pleased him so much. If nothing comes from that direction, there is nothing more to hope for. The disappointment is all the greater because so much had been hoped." Goya did not even get paid for a long time.

If the prime minister let Goya down, the Infante Don Luis Antonio de Borbón, younger brother of King Charles III, took him up. Probably Goya had been introduced to the prince by Ventura Rodríguez.

Don Luis had been made a cardinal when he was only ten years old, and given sees which yielded him an enormous revenue. After his father, Ferdinand VI, died, he decided he was tired of enforced celibacy. He resigned his offices and, being pleasure-loving rather than ambitious, pressed no claim for the throne of Spain, to which he had a better right than his brother Charles. For a wife he settled on the beautiful Doña Maria Teresa de Vallabriga, daughter of a proud and ancient Aragon family, but without royal blood in her veins. The morganatic marriage Charles III sanctioned, but he banished his brother and sister-in-law from Court as a punishment.

It was no hardship for the Infante Luis, who gladly retired to his lavish country estate at Los Arenas de San Pedro, in the province of Avila. There he pursued his favorite diversions of botany, art, music, and hunting. He even abandoned the scandalously profligate life he had led as a prince of the Church and became a responsible married man.

In the late summer of 1783, the infante summoned Goya to Los Arenas to paint portraits of his family in this tranquil domestic environment. The prince liked Goya, especially since Goya loved hunting as much as he did and was even better at it. Goya had a wonderful time for the month he was with the family.

They apparently enjoyed him too, for they made him promise to return every year. When he left, he was not only paid promptly, with a bonus to boot, but given a dress "all in gold and silver" for Josefa. The "little dauber," as the infante affectionately called him, was ecstatic. "They are angels, these princes!" he wrote Zapater. He was peasant enough, for all his entertainment by royalty, to ask the servants of the wardrobe how much Josefa's gown was worth. When they told him—about $1,250—he was flabbergasted. As a farewell present he gave the family still lifes he had painted of the game he and the infante had shot.

In the short time he was at Los Arenas he painted five portraits. One he says he executed in an hour on August 27; another, in three hours on September 11. Probably he meant the faces alone. He was working independently at last, expressing as much of his own vision as he then understood. This freedom, plus the lift his stay gave his self-

Maria Teresa de Borbón
y Vallabriga. *National
Gallery of Art, Wash-
ington, D.C.*
PHOTO MAS, BARCELONA

esteem, restored to him the old speed and sureness of touch
he seems to have lacked in the Floridablanca portrait.

The most charming of these family portraits is that of
the two-year-old Maria Teresa de Borbón y Vallabriga, the
prince's daughter. Technically, however, it is almost primitive. The terrace on which the child is standing is stiff and
formal. The drawing is tight, and details are overempha-
sized. The dancing-school pose of the princess is artificial.
Still she expresses the sweetness of childhood, and an innocence that becomes poignant in view of the unhappy life
the little girl was to have, as shown in the portrait Goya

83

made of her seventeen years later, when she was the Countess of Chinchón.

The group portrait Goya did of the family of the infante and their servants is less successful. His provinciality shows in the way he gives these aristocrats the quality of a bourgeois household that thinks their intimate doings of interest to the world.

Goya's visit to Los Arenas had helped him discern the sophistication of persons always able to get anything they wanted and escape getting anything they did not want. Much as Goya could share the infante's passion for hunting, he could perceive that the prince's values were different. Even the game they brought in had been bred and positioned for no other purpose than their "sport."

Goya was beginning to understand how much he had to learn about people. Or were these pampered nobles, he wondered, real people? Perhaps the glint of their jewels and of their gold and silver gowns was falser than the glitter of the *majos'* and *majas'* tinsel. Floridablanca had treated him like an underling; perhaps the people at Los Arenas, kind and generous as they were, regarded him also as a hireling to be patronized rather than accepted. The dress for Josefa was a gorgeous thing, but where in the world could she wear it without appearing ridiculous? But, oh, how useful this connection would be!

Goya was back in Madrid by September 20, exhausted. He soon relapsed from his elation over his social progress into his previous mood of despondency. "I feel depressed," he wrote Zapater, "and I am not doing much work. I have not even finished the equestrian portrait of the infante." He was looking forward to the unveiling of the San Francisco el Grande picture.

Preoccupations with his family had brought him back to earth after the carefree luxury of Los Arenas. His brother Camillo either wanted to enter the Church, or Goya thought the Church the only possible career for him. In 1781, he had written Zapater: "For Camillo I am hoping he will go to Toledo to see whether God wills that he may be a priest. If he [God or Camillo?] does not, we will think up something for him here, so that he can find something to do." He seemed relieved that his brother Tomás, at least, had found work as a gilder like their father.

The problem of Camillo led Goya to test the friendship of the Infante Luis. The prince responded by getting Camillo a chaplaincy at Chinchón, a town about twenty miles southeast of Madrid. This patronage infuriated Goya's enemies, whoever they were. Camillo was installed by October, 1784, for on the eighteenth of that month he wrote to Martín Zapater his own none-too-perceptive opinions of his brother's state of mind.

"I cannot give you the kind of news I would like about Francho," Camillo wrote. "Although God has endowed him with good luck and ability, they have persecuted him so that he has lost patience. This is their revenge for not being able to damage his reputation. They criticize everything he says or does not say, and misrepresent its meaning. I am so upset that I cannot say what I really want to. The worst of it all is that they are making him hate painting. They cannot make him give it up, but they do make him loath to continue. The reason is that they cannot bear to see him get so much praise and honor from everyone but themselves."

What Camillo failed to see was that Goya was dissatisfied with himself. He could not brave poverty and obscurity to indulge his dream of what he could do if he were free of the necessity of conforming to the taste of his time. Nor could he give up the image he had created for himself

85

as the poor peasant boy who had made good in the big city. It was impossible for him to find a synthesis between the ideals that were pulling him in opposite directions.

Practical considerations proved more important to him than dreams, now that he had to take care of his widowed mother. He had brought the old lady to live with him in Madrid in September, 1783. She was miserable there, away from her old friends, and helpless in the turmoil of the capital after the quiet simplicity of Fuendetodos and Zaragoza. Her son's house was not hers. She pleaded to go home. Goya let her, probably with a sense that he had failed again. He gave her an allowance for the rest of her life.

Gone was the gay tone of his letter to Zapater of 1778, in which he made fun, in Andalusian dialect, of Martín's opinions of the star *toreros:* "Nonsense, old boy! You make me laugh!"—followed by twenty "ha-ha-ha's" occupying two and a half lines. Goya would not have been so extravagant with letter paper now. He began writing his friend on the unused parts of Zapater's letters, and filling up any blanks with flourishes. "Now," he added coarsely, "you can (not) use this paper (to write on)." Goya was equally economical with canvas, using old pieces already painted on, or the back of a piece on which he had sketched another subject.

At last, in November, 1784, came the unveiling of the paintings which had been commissioned for the Church of San Francisco el Grande. It had been delayed because of deaths among the royal children. Goya wrote to Zapater that "talking about the altarpieces has begun, and a good deal of it." It was clear that Goya had surpassed his competitors. He was ecstatic. A few days later, on December 4, he wrote again: "At present we are in the excitement of the paintings of San Francisco, and, thanks to God, the comments go on as they began."

Four days later, on Wednesday, December 8, the king and his Court came to the church to see the paintings. Goya's was in a side chapel beside the Gospel. It attracted all the attention. On December 11, Goya wrote: "I have been fortunate not only with the critics but with the public also. The king himself praised the picture before the whole Court and the members of the Academy."

Goya had chosen as his subject "St. Bernardino of Siena Preaching before King Alfonso V of Aragon." The saint, who lived from 1380 to 1444, was a famous Franciscan preacher of sermons that lasted for hours but which were remarkably lively. How Goya chose this subject and why is unknown; probably it was suggested to him by some learned monk, or it may have been assigned. If Goya had done his own research, he might have found a more suitable incident in the life of the saint, who was credited with many miracles and who instigated many "bonfires of vanities," any one of which would have made a more dramatic subject.

The painting has not borne out the judgment of the critics of Goya's day. It is static and dull, and overcrowded with two detailed figures, one of whom is Goya himself in a fifteenth-century costume (at the far right). The saint, who stands on a rock, is topped by a very literal star that makes him look rather like a Christmas tree.

Goya had a hard time collecting the money due him for the *St. Bernardino*. Finally he, along with Gregorio Ferro and José del Castillo, two other competitors, had to petition the prime minister. They called his attention to the long time they had spent on the work at their own expense, emphasizing that they were not salaried Court Painters— a broad hint that they should be. The secretary of the Academy of San Fernando seconded their petition on the grounds that "these poor fellows" would be stimulated to more and better work if they were to be paid.

San Bernardino of Siena. *San Francisco el Grande, Madrid.*

Floridablanca eventually authorized payment. With a critical sense beyond that of his time he scrawled on the margin of the document: "None of the pictures is worth much, but those of these men are the least bad."

The year 1784 ended happily for Goya. On December 2, Josefa had presented him with his third son, Francisco Javier Pedro. "Healthy and robust," Javier, as he was to be known, lived until 1854.

5

Kings and Princes

Goya's association with the Infante Don Luis and his family brought him more than a chaplaincy for Camillo. After his return to the capital in the early autumn of 1783, Goya began getting commissions from other grandees and ministers of state. The most important came from the Osuna family, who were among the "enlightened"—that is, progressive—of the aristocracy. As if to imitate the prince of the blood, they invited Goya to their summer palace, the Alameda, then known as *El Capricho,* in the flatlands of Castile, south of Madrid.

It was a region almost deserted, for the Duke of Osuna owned such vast areas that no towns could flourish, and independent farming was impossible. These lands brought the duke the equivalent of between three and four million dollars a year, which required twenty-nine accountants to handle. Even so, he was in debt, for he lived in magnificence.

Don Pedro de Alcantaro, Marquis of Peñafiel and ninth Duke of Osuna (1755–1807), had a reputation for sensitivity, knowledge, and ambition rare for a Spanish nobleman of that time, especially for one of his exalted family. He collected an excellent library, having got royal permission to import books forbidden by the Inquisition. This he was public-spirited enough to bequeath to the Spanish people, but the Inquisition forbade that gift. So far as Goya was concerned, its chief attraction was the fifty fine French prints the duke had collected in France, which Goya could study. Goya found his host kindly and generous and placid.

The Duchess of Osuna may have possessed the first two of those qualities, but she was anything but placid. A first cousin of her husband, she was twice a princess herself and several times a countess. The power-hungry blood of the Borgias ran in her veins, mixed with that of more ancient and more refined families. She was the epitome of the pride and arrogance of the Spanish aristocrats, but she was far from effete. Risks and actual dangers she despised. She would go off on long horseback rides alone, sleeping wherever she could. Disguised as a sailor, she went with her husband to the siege of Minorca, in August, 1781, in which he commanded the division of the fleet which captured the fort at Fornells.

Maria Josefa Pimentel Téllez Girón y Borja, Countess-Duchess of Benevente, Duchess of Osuna, wished to shine in other fields as well. Not for her was the well-nigh illiterate ignorance of the Spanish woman of all classes. The duchess could talk and write with intelligence and grace, and she understood finance well enough to manage the income from her vast estates, which were greater than the duke's. She even got herself elected President of the Women's Section of the Economics Society of Madrid, and lectured to large audiences on the intricacies of the science, which was being developed in France. She adored all things and ideas French.

Lady Holland, the wife of the British ambassador to Spain, said the duchess was "the most distinguished lady in Madrid for her talents, worth, and taste." She also wrote that the duchess' vivacity made up for "her total want of refinement and acquirement," and that she was "rather imperious in her family."

Lady Holland may have been envious. The Duchess of

Osuna was a patron of literature and art and music. Her *tertulias*—the evening parties of the time which were devoted to discussion of some intellectual topic—attracted poets, painters, and composers. She even maintained a little theater for which Tomás de Iriarte wrote several of his stylish verse plays. The duchess herself sometimes acted in them.

The duchess' patronage of Goya, which perhaps began as early as 1783, was a great step upward for his social ambitions. He spent considerable time during the next ten years at the Alameda, and produced some good work for the family.

In 1785 he painted the duchess' portrait in a style in keeping with the Osunas' preference for the simplicity advocated by the new philosophy of the day. He saw her as cool, tense, overbred. The infinitely subtle flicker of a smile on her thin, pale lips betrays a kind of degenerate cruelty. It is a masterful representation of a masterful woman. Goya was finding himself at last as a sardonic commentator on a decadent society. The most damaging error these aristocrats made was to let the shrewd peasant from Aragon know them too well.

Much later, probably in 1798, Goya painted the Duke of Osuna. This portrait now hangs in the Frick Collection, in New York City. One glance at it is enough for the spectator to understand that the duke was a great aristocrat and at the same time an understanding man. Whereas his wife's lips are almost sneering, his are parted in a humorous smile.

Besides portraits, Goya painted several genre pieces for the Osunas, much in the style and of the subject matter he chose for his second set of tapestry cartoons, which he began in 1786. These show his preoccupation with the common people, their sufferings, and their hardships. In

The Duchess of Osuna.
*Collection of D. J.
March, Palma de Mallorca.*

The Duke of Osuna.
*Copyright The Frick
Collection, New York.*

Winter, five peasants, muffled against an icy wind, are leading a loaded donkey through a bleak, snow-covered mountain pass. They ache from cold and fatigue. The bare branches of a tree bent toward them show how the wind bites into their faces. The only cheering notes are the reds, blues, and yellows of their clothing, as if to prove their fortitude.

The duke, whose revenues came largely from agriculture, no doubt appreciated Goya's rural scenes, but it would be interesting to know what he thought of the six paintings of witchcraft and sorcery Goya later supplied to decorate his country palace. Probably these were done to please the duchess. There was a current revival of necromancy in Madrid high circles that may have suggested them. Or they may be scenes from the plays the duchess fancied; at least one of them certainly is.

A belief in witchcraft has always been part of the Spanish character. As late as 1934 the residents of Hospitalet, a suburb of Barcelona, had one of their neighbors indicted as a witch after supplying a judge with startling evidence of her conjuring.

The Witches' Sabbath (*Aquelarre*) is the most astonishing of these weird scenes. A great he-goat, personifying the Devil, his long, lyre-shaped horns festooned with a garland possibly made of poison ivy, presides over a coven of nine hideous hags who are offering him the dead bodies of emaciated infants. In the background three of these hang from a pole like a string of fish. Enormous bats swoop through a baleful sky illumined by a waning moon.

It would be reassuring to believe the whole picture a joke, but it seems to be an expression of Goya's feeling that behind the world he saw lurked another, peopled with evil monsters. He was objectifying his sense of persecution. The personal, human enemies he believed were plotting to

Witches' Sabbath, painted for the Duke and Duchess of Osuna.
Lazaro Galdiano Museum, Madrid.

ruin him became the creatures of a Satanic netherworld.
His foes now are not individuals but the whole threat of
the ruin of man's soul by the invisible forces of evil.

A good man, Goya is saying, casts the shadow of a devil.
A beautiful woman conceals a witch's soul. Beneath every
action hides a wicked, destructive motive. Innocent, beautiful children are born only to be shriveled and devoured
by the horrors of life.

These symbols keep appearing in Goya's work from this
time on. Just as he was learning to see through the span-

95

gled gauze of the Court into its decadence and corruption, so he was seeing more in life itself than the pretty masquerades of the tapestry cartoons. Thought was intruding on decoration.

This sardonic point of view appears in Goya's portrait of General Manuel Lapeña Ruiz del Saltillo, Marquis of Bondad Real. Painted in 1799, it yet belongs in the group of Osuna paintings, for the marquis was the Duchess of Osuna's *cortejo*, and she probably ordered the portrait, which now hangs in the Hispanic Society of America, New York City.

The institution of the *cortejo* was another aspect of the sophistication of the Spanish aristocracy. A *cortejo* was usually married himself, but attached himself to a married woman of the upper class and became her constant escort. The two were bound less by emotional ties, though these sometimes figured in the relationship, than by social convenience. The duchess and Lapeña's wife, for example, were apparently good friends. It was not too convenient for the man, however, for he was put to enormous expense in maintaining, as it were, two households. Goya, the practical peasant, saw the whole business as ridiculous.

General Lapeña is reported to have been "incapable of a swift and heroic decision, a selfish colleague, and a disloyal subordinate," and possessed of "an excess of caution." Goya's opinion coincides with these judgments. (The Duchess of Osuna may have thought differently; at least she made Lapeña executor of her will.) The portrait reveals a gorgeously uniformed military boob, full of conceit and hence quite uninterested in his profession. A soldier-doll himself, the detached general is satirized by the little troop of "tin" soldiers drilling in the background under their laden clotheslines. The military barracks are placed so far away that they, too, seem like toys in comparison with the life-size figure of Lapeña.

The Marquis of Bondad Real. *Courtesy of the Hispanic Society of America, New York.*

The Osunas were by no means Goya's only clients. He was besieged with orders for portraits, and his studio became a veritable workshop. The speedy technique he had developed stood him in good stead, for he had to work fast in order to keep up with the commissions. He is said to have permitted no talking from his sitters. If they broke the rule, Goya would throw down his brushes and his palette, and sometimes would not paint for days after the interruption. His son Javier remembered that his father painted "in one session only, which sometimes lasted up to ten hours, but never in the evening; and in order to

97

heighten the effect of a portrait, he added the final touches at night under artificial light."

A self-portrait Goya painted at this period (see cover) bears out Javier's recollection. Goya is standing before his easel in a shadowy studio. Behind him is a lighted window. On the brim of his hat is a ring of candle holders. Apparently he used a maulstick to steady his hand for detailed work, for one appears on his business card held by the magpie in his portrait of Don Manuel Osorio de Zúñiga.

Javier's note hardly means that Goya's sitters posed for ten hours. Queen Maria Luisa, who sat for him in the fall of 1799, wrote: "The portrait . . . has been completed in three sittings. . . . I spent two hours and a half on a raised platform . . . so that Goya could go on with what he was doing."

Many of Goya's portraits were developed from sketches in color or chalk made previously of the sitter in person; these were later completed from costumes loaned to Goya. He employed assistants from time to time, but only for allegorical and religious paintings. The only pupil known to have touched Goya's work was Dionisio Gomez. No one could equal Goya's extraordinary brushwork in painting lace, embroidery, the texture of silk and satin, the glitter of jewels and military decorations, or the transparency of veils.

F. Schmid has made a detailed analysis of Goya's technique. First, Goya covered his surface with a red-orange or tanned-leather ground—the underpainting. On this he sketched the outline of the figure with ivory black. The flesh tints he laid directly on the reddish ground, matching them to the subject's own coloring. The modeling was done with ivory black or raw umber. Middle tints are greenish or grayish; shadows are pure ivory black.

Goya mixed his tints from the colors on his palette, using

a palette knife to get a clean paste that matched the colors he saw. This paste gives the flesh in Goya's portraits its characteristic brilliancy. Everything was done while all the paint was wet; hence the softness of Goya's brushwork. A fine example of this is Goya's portrait of Josefa Castillo de Portugal de Garcini, in the Metropolitan Museum of Art, New York City.

Schmid's reconstruction of Goya's palette shows its arrangement and the colors he used:

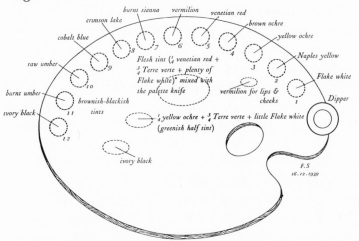

*To which may be added a little yellow ochre or vermilion or burnt sienna or crimson lake or raw umber to match the complexion of the sitter

Goya's palette, as reconstructed by F. Schmid from the portrait of Goya by Vicente Lopez.

The light and the middle flesh tints Goya applied with hog-bristle brushes. Sometimes these two tints were joined with clean sable's hair pencils. After the surface was dry, Goya varnished it with mastic or Venetian turpentine. Then he glazed the shadows with a sponge, working the colors—asphaltum, crimson lake, yellow lake—into the varnish. In his later work he sometimes applied his paint with a palette knife, a rag wrapped around a stick, or a spoon handle, and he used the palm of his hand or his thumb for expressive touches.

Frequently, especially in his later work, Goya used a technique called scumbling. This is an application of an opaque or semiopaque layer of paint over an underlayer, either lighter or darker. It obscures the underpainting, but does not conceal it. In the *City on a Rock*, in New York's Metropolitan Museum of Art, Goya scumbled lighter colors over a darker ground with a palette knife. The procedure reveals the weave of the canvas, which becomes part of the paint quality. The effect contributes to the beauty of the work.

To please his sitters, Goya was still following the French fashion in pose, costume, and background. The portrait of the Marquesa de Pontejos, in the National Gallery of Art, Washington, D. C., for example, is really a French fashion plate. The lady was Floridablanca's sister-in-law, and apparently Goya's portrait is a "wedding photograph," completed at the time of her marriage in 1786. She was a member of the Duchess of Osuna's Women's Economics Society, though probably a silent one, for her catlike face is charming but unintelligent.

Here the colors are the same silvery pinks and greens and lavenders of Goya's tapestry cartoons. They give the painting a candy-box tone, which the artificially pretty landscape and the stilted pose of the marquesa complement. All the vapidity of a fragile age that was soon to end in violence appears in this delightful satire. It is a last glimpse at a never-never-world too elegant and dainty to wish to see the ruin just ahead of it.

Also to this period belongs one of Goya's most popular paintings—the portrait of Don Manuel Osorio Manrique de Zúñiga, in the Metropolitan Museum of Art, New York City. The irresistible little black-eyed, auburn-haired

Don Manuel Osorio. *The Metropolitan Museum of Art, New York, Jules S. Bache Collection.*

boy must have delighted Goya's heart. It is the first of his portraits—its date is 1788 or '89—in which his unique personality is unmistakably clear. Compare it, for instance, with the conventional pose and décor of the portrait of Maria Teresa de Borbón, in which Goya was following the prescriptions of Mengs and Bayeu.

Few paintings express so well the joy the artist got out of executing them. Goya was plainly much amused by his tiny sitter showing off his tame magpie's tricks under the sinister eyes of three monstrous cats eager to pounce on the bird. The cats, which were to turn up again in Goya's savagely satirical *Caprichos,* seem to represent here the dangers lying ahead for the unsuspecting child.

The portrait of Don Manuel shows the qualities of mind and heart which Goya had long been striving to express: tenderness, humor, pathos, prophecy, the truth of nature, the fallacy of sophistication. The portrait is a superb piece of painting—the skillful brushwork of the filmy lace collar, the gleam of the satin sash with its elaborate bow one can almost hear rustle. Flashes of light in the cats' eyes and in the red and yellow flecks of the caged birds' plumage animate passages not illuminated by the boy's vermilion suit. It is a fine example of Goya's theory that the business of art is to capture the vibrancy of life suspended for but the briefest moment.

Goya also painted Don Manuel's brother, the ten-year-old Vicente, Count of Trastamara, in 1786 or '87. The portrait is now in the collection of Mrs. Charles S. Payson, New York City. Here the rapport between artist and sitter was not so complete. The work still shows the influence on Goya of Mengs and Bayeu. Although Goya catches the irony of the timid little boy in his powdered wig and elegant small clothes, with his hand on a sword hilt, the portrait lacks true originality.

The two boys were the sons of the Count and Countess

of Altamira, of one of the oldest and most distinguished families in Spain. They had taken Goya up, as had the Infante Don Luis and the Osunas, and he had painted the count and his wife.

The count's portrait was finished in 1787 for the newly established national bank of Spain, the Bank of San Carlos, of which the count was a director, and it hangs there now. The bank had been founded by the eminent financier, François Cabarrus, in 1781; it was the most important economic foundation of the reform period under Charles III. Goya had at least fifteen shares in it, and attended the shareholders' meeting in 1787.

Goya apparently saw little to admire in the count, who was so short of stature as to be ridiculous. The king is supposed to have teased him about his height, only to be told by the haughty aristocrat that he might seem very little at Court, but that on his estates he was very big indeed. Goya placed him at a table almost as high as the count himself, and did nothing to disguise his smug banality; in fact, he emphasizes it by discordant reds, yellows, and blues. When Goya was bored by a sitter, as he often was by these pretentious aristocrats, he did boring work.

The countess' portrait, in the collection of Robert Lehman, of New York City, is again in the French style, like that of the Marquesa de Pontejos. This was probably painted in late 1787, for the countess holds her daughter Maria Augustina, who is under a year old and who was born on February 21, 1787. Both the elegantly dressed woman and the baby are stiff and staring, symbols rather than flesh-and-blood creatures. Again appear the same French pastel colors of pink and blue and silvery gray, and the same tight, academic drawing. Apparently Goya did not fit in with the Altamira family so congenially as with his other noble patrons.

In general, the portraits Goya painted during this period

of his development reveal him as skeptical of the values of the aristocracy and cynical about the supposed nobility of human nature. He was still struggling to integrate his personality. The more success came to him, the more violently he seems inwardly to have fought the sources of it.

Outwardly he was as aggressive as ever. In 1785, after the death of Andrea Calleja, he sought again the distinction he coveted, and applied for Calleja's post as Court Painter. His candidacy, he wrote Zapater, was an open secret at Court, but he was too superstitious to talk about it until he had been chosen. Perhaps he had already talked too much and too optimistically. The king turned him down.

Nevertheless, Charles III could not overlook the fact that Goya was now the most brilliant and fashionable portrait painter in his land. When the Bank of San Carlos requested a portrait of the king and recommended the painter from whom they had ordered portraits of their directors and principal stockholders, Charles consented to sit for Goya.

Goya painted him twice. The first portrait, done in late 1786 (it was paid for on January 29, 1787), showing the king in Court dress, hangs in the bank, in Madrid. The other, painted probably a year later, hangs in the Prado, and is the more famous. Patterned after Velázquez' well-known portrait of Philip IV in hunting dress, this one catches Charles III at his favorite diversion. The king seems to have had a good day with his gun, for he is smiling, and the dog at his feet is tired from retrieving his quarry. Or perhaps the monarch, who had not much longer to live, could not help being amused at the painter whose personality had pleased so many of his grandees.

The greatness of the portrait, however, lies in its total honesty. Not a trace of idealism mars this vision of an old

King Charles III of Spain. *Prado Museum, Madrid.*

PHOTO MAS, BARCELONA

man, weary of responsibility and exhausted by disappointments. His legs are thin and bowed; his drooping shoulders bent; his wrinkled face, with sunken eyes and enormously long nose, is rather like a vulture's. Yet, in spite of
its comic aspects, the figure has dignity, for the angles of
the king's hat and of his gun set everything straight and
solemn. In its revelation of the kind of personality that
often wields the power of this world it equals the great
portraits of prelates by Raphael and Titian, Velázquez and
El Greco.

Goya never mentioned these two royal portraits to
Zapater. It is barely possible that they were not painted
from life. But he wrote with his usual exaggeration about
the consolation for his failing to become a Court Painter.
He had been elected to Calleja's former position as Assistant Director of the Academy of San Fernando, and the
king had approved. "Little profit but much honor," was
Goya's comment. Now he had a position of power in the
art world of Spain. And the post was the equal of Bayeu's.

"Profit" was becoming a matter of some concern to
Goya. By 1786 he was earning the equivalent of about
$750 a year, out of which he could save enough to make
some investments. He wrote Zapater that he was "the most
contented and happiest man in the world."

A laborer's income then was about $10 a year. Goya
could have hired all the inhabitants of Fuendetodos, and
raised their wages. Still he complained to Zapater that his
expenses were heavy because of the position in society he
had reached. He could not, or would not, cut them. "I
am very well known here," Goya added, "but I am not so
well off as people think." Always the prudent peasant, he
was panicky about a possible lean harvest. It angered him
to be asked for a loan.

He was also a newly rich peasant, and so he had to show
off his good fortune. A carriage of one's own was the best

way to do this in Madrid. Anything to avoid using the calashes and the chaises and the wretchedly uncomfortable sedan chairs that could be rented in the Plazuela de la Cebada. These were the principal means the less prosperous citizens had of getting about the filthy streets of the capital.

So Goya bought himself a stylish two-wheeled cabriolet of English design, and a ten-year-old horse to pull it. The first time he tried it out, he took along the horse dealer, a Neapolitan. Everyone in the streets stopped to stare at them; there were only two other vehicles like Goya's in Madrid. The man said he would show Goya how the fashionable Neapolitans turned around without checking their speed.

Goya was only too ready to learn this trick of fine driving. But the Italian was not so adept as he claimed. The carriage turned over, landing horse and occupants in a ditch. Goya broke his right leg and was lame for several months.

The next time he took the rig out, he ran over a pedestrian, incurring a heavy penalty. So he traded the cabriolet for a sober four-wheeled carriage, and commissioned Zapater secretly to find him two docile mules to pull it. "What would people in Zaragoza say if they knew the mules were for me!" He recognized his pride and prayed for the strength to check it.

He was also writing to Zapater to do some genealogical research on the Lucientes family. If it could be proved that Goya's mother really was an *hidalga,* then her son could add a "de" to his name. The peasant would become a patrician. A 1784 letter to Goya from the brilliant lawyer and state official Jovellanos is addressed: "Don Francisco de Goya," as if to tease the artist for his pretentiousness when he himself pretended to hate pretension.

He was dressing fashionably, too, and having his hair

curled by a barber like all the other dandies of Madrid. Madrileños spent an unconscionable amount of time at the hairdressers. He kept his shirts fresh, and had ruffles added to their collars and cuffs. The vanity which made him react so savagely to criticism of his work shows up in his costume and the many portraits he painted of himself in it.

In June, 1786, "by the order of the King," at which he was very proud, Goya undertook a second series of cartoons for tapestries to be manufactured at the Royal Tapestry Manufactory. These were destined for the apartments in the Escorial of the king's son, the Infante Gabriel, who had just married Doña Maria Ana Victoria de Braganza, a princess of Portugal. At least two of the seven contracted for were finished by that autumn.

For subjects Goya chose the four seasons. They show the daily life of rural Spain in a more realistic fashion than the first series of ten years before. One, *Winter,* is almost the same as the version Goya painted for the Duke of Osuna's Alameda palace (page 109). The same emphasis on the hard life of the poor appears in two others: *A Poor Family at a Well* and *The Injured Bricklayer.* The former tends to be a sentimental anecdote, but the latter is a dramatic expression of the dignity of work, its hazards, its miseries. Goya was introducing a note of social comment, as if to caution the newlyweds that their pomp and power and wealth were got at a price.

Also to this series belongs the charming *Boy on a Ram,* in the McCormick Collection, Chicago, another of Goya's wholly realistic representations of children. Its cool blues and whites, and the silhouette of the figure against a simple background, show Goya's more sophisticated approach to composition and color than that of the earlier series.

The work interested Goya little. Even the money he got for it was small. The larger cartoons brought him the equiv-

The Injured Bricklayer, one of Goya's second series of tapestry cartoons. *Prado Museum, Madrid.*

alent of about $440 each; the smaller ones, about half that. Still he kept on with it as a security against the time when portrait commissions might not be so plentiful. He remained so busy that he never got time to execute a Madonna he had promised Martín Zapater as a consolation for the death of his dear friend's father.

Religious painting, as a matter of fact, interested Goya even less; yet he did it whenever he got an order. In 1784 Jovellanos got him a commission for four paintings for the College of Calatrava in Salamanca. These were destroyed during the Peninsular War, and only their subjects are known: *The Immaculate Conception, St. Bernard, St. Benedict, St. Raymond of Penaforte*. It is safe to assume that they were no more distinguished than Goya's other work in this field, of which he had no deep understanding.

The following year he did an *Annunciation* for the Duke of Medinaceli, which was installed in the Church of San Antonio del Prado, Madrid, on December 8, 1785. This, too, is derivative of the Italian baroque style, and conventional.

Goya's first good work in religious painting appeared in the series of altarpieces he painted for the Convent Church of St. Joaquin and Santa Ana in Valladolid, about eighty-five miles northwest of Madrid. These had been ordered by Charles III in early June, 1787, with the stipulation that they be finished by July 26. Goya, who regarded them as potboilers, had no intention of not completing them by then, and he did so. Naturally his haste ruined the quality of two of them—mere sentimental, life-size, conventional saints: St. Bernard again, with St. Robert; and St. Lutgard, the blind Flemish mystic of the thirteenth century. Above St. Bernard's head, as he gives communion to a cripple, shines a star, as in the *San Bernardino Preaching*, giving him the same Christmas tree appearance. But the *Death of St. Joseph*, for all it is influenced by the baroque Carlo Maratti and the rococo Giuseppe Maria Crespi, is strong and original. Here Goya seems to be searching for a new way to express himself by using light to suggest mysticism and at the same time keep his figures realistic.

This advance is also noticeable in two paintings commissioned by the Duchess of Osuna, for which Goya billed her on October 16, 1788. Perhaps he was working on them as early as May 31, and with greater interest now that he had found a satisfactory means of expression for religious themes. For on that date he wrote Zapater that he hoped

St. Francisco Borgia at the Deathbed of an Impenitent. *Cathedral, Valencia.*

III

"God would let us live for His holy service." The works were intended for a chapel the duchess had constructed in the Cathedral of Valencia and dedicated to the saint of her family, the Marquis of Lombay (1510–72).

This nobleman had been designated by Charles V to take the corpse of the emperor's beautiful first wife, Isabel of Portugal, to Granada for burial. When the coffin was opened there for identification of its occupant, the decomposed body so impressed the marquis with the vanity of this world that he became a Jesuit in 1546. He was later canonized as St. Francisco Borgia.

Goya avoided depicting the saint's conversion, something he did not understand or relish. Instead he chose two other incidents from the saint's life: his leave-taking of his family, and his exhortation of a dying man to repent. They are rendered in a vivid theatrical style. The first is a scene of pathos. The weeping young marquis stands on the steps of the Borgia palace illuminated by light from above the staircase. In the second, which was influenced by Houasse's *Miracle of St. Francis de Regis,* light is focused, as by a spotlight, on the saint as he stands by the deathbed. The dying man is powerfully painted. He gasps and groans in the agony of expiring; even his feet express his torture. Goya painted the figure naked, but the cathedral authorities objected, and hired some now-unknown painter to cover it with a sheet.

At the dying man's head are demons and monsters leering powerlessly at the saint's bleeding crucifix. It is the first of many times these creatures would appear in Goya's work.

At last Goya had mastered the problem of a religious subject simply by exploring its human side. The whole dramatic scene cannot help impressing the spectator with the strong conflicts among its elements. Clashes of cold color emphasize these.

The conflicts were an intensification of those in Goya's soul. His strong desires and ambitions had made him popular in high society. He was captivated with it, proud of the long way he had come from the miserable hut in Fuendetodos. He could write to Zapater in 1786: "My life is enviable. I never have to sit in waiting rooms. If anyone wants me, he must come to me. If a client is not a distinguished personage or recommended by one I know, I will not work for him. Still I get more clients than I can satisfy."

On the other hand, he was only occasionally able truly to express himself. The basic scorn he had for the life he had entered kept creeping into his work. Physical and nervous exhaustion from incessant painting aggravated this feeling. By May, 1787, he was complaining to Zapater that Josefa was sick, the cook was sick, and the sick baby was worse. The child was the beloved Javier—Josefa had had a miscarriage on August 5, 1785, which seems to have ended her productivity—and Goya was frantic.

In December of the same year he wrote: "I have grown old and have many wrinkles. You would not recognize me except for my flat nose and sunken eyes. I feel every one of my forty-one years, but you probably are still as young-looking as when we were at Father Joaquin's school."

Actually Goya, if his self-portraits can be trusted, looked young for his age. But trouble was brewing. The cold war of his emotions was close to flaring into a conflict that would almost destroy him.

6

Triumph and Disaster

Charles III of Spain died in the early morning of December 14, 1788. The funeral ceremonies were as detailed and precise as the king's schedule had been. While church bells tolled, the nobles dressed their late sovereign in his ceremonial robes and decorations, placed the body in a wooden coffin covered with cloth of gold, laid that inside a leaden casket, and carried him to the Hall of Ambassadors, where the weeping public could pay their last homage. Goya himself probably filed past the soldiers of the king's guard to take a final look at the face he had made more enduring than nature had.

The next day the body was taken to the Escorial, where, after five years in the "rotting room," it would lie amongst its predecessors in the pantheon of Spanish monarchs. The captain of the king's guard broke his staff of office. Charles IV was then officially King of Spain. He was crowned in January, 1789.

Thus the best of the Bourbons was followed by one of the worst. Charles IV was stupid, weak, and dissolute. The best thing that can be said of him is that he liked music; he even pretended to play the violin in a Court ensemble while a more accomplished fiddler rendered the king's part from behind a screen. He also dabbled in painting, and presumed to offer the Academy some of his and his wife's efforts with the brush.

Among the first acts of the new king were the restoration of bullfighting, which his father had suppressed in 1785, and the appointment of Goya as Court Painter in April, 1789. Both acts pleased the painter immensely.

Charles IV's queen, Maria Luisa, liked Goya. Frequently she would invite him to breakfast for the sake of his conversation. This meant that the king liked him, and that Manuel Godoy, the queen's lover, soon to be prime minister, liked him. Maria Luisa ran the Court as she wished, and almost ran the country too.

When Maria Luisa was a child, her young brother struck her while they were playing. Since she was already engaged to her cousin Charles, and knew what her future position would be, she furiously reminded her brother that she was entitled to obeisance, not abuse. "Oh, well," the boy said, "at least I can say some day that I have slapped the queen of Spain."

Maria Luisa might have profited from several sound slappings. As soon as she married Charles at the age of not quite fifteen, she began to dominate him—a relatively easy task except for his impotent rages of stupidity which once in a great while subdued her temporarily. She was flagrantly unfaithful to him, as everyone but he knew. He refused to believe it. He thought Maria Luisa was wonderful.

Old Charles III had been shrewd enough to see his daughter-in-law for what she was—evil, cruel, sly, and sensual. He kept her out of sight and out of power. Probably he was the only person who was ever able to do so. As soon as he was dead, Maria Luisa made up for this ignominy. Under her leadership the Court threw off its stiff propriety along with its mourning for the late king, and became as abandoned as Maria Luisa herself.

For the queen had already grown old, as her husband

sometimes reminded her teasingly. (His playfulness was brutal; a "friendly" slap on the back from him often sent the recipient reeling, and howling with pain.) She covered her flabby cheeks with rouge till she looked like a harridan, and she kept three dentists constantly at Court to repair and adjust the complete set of false teeth she had to wear. She was determined to make up for lost time.

To that end she used what assets she had. She was intelligent, and shrewd at handling people. She was brave, and firm in her decisions. She had a gift for organization and for keeping loyalties. And she could put people at ease so graciously that sometimes they failed to suspect her baser nature and designs.

All these qualities Charles IV lacked. He would have been lost without Maria Luisa. As it turned out, he was lost with her. For she failed to instill any filial affection in the children born of her loveless marriage, and her eldest son destroyed both his parents.

Such were Goya's new patrons, and such was the atmosphere of the highest level of Spanish society into which he at last had been admitted. As Court Painter he could come and go as he pleased, and it pleased him, after so many years of envious longing, to do so regularly.

By September 21, 1789, when the new monarchs made their ceremonial entry into the capital city after the period of mourning for Charles III was over, Goya had painted Charles IV and Maria Luisa at least twice. The portraits were intended for the illuminated displays in honor of the occasion that the Duchess of Osuna and the Duke of Hyar erected before their palaces. All the decorations throughout the city were splendid. Dancing went on all night in the mansions and in the public squares.

Two months earlier in another capital, north of the Pyrenees, a different kind of dancing was going on in the public squares. A mob had sacked and burned the Bastille, that dungeon fortress-symbol of royal absolutism and oppression. A people drunk with their first taste of political freedom reeled through the carmagnole in the St.-Antoine quarter of Paris. A few sensitive ears might have heard its echoes in Madrid's Plaza del Armería and sensed a grim undertone in the welcome of the city to the new sovereigns. Crowned Bourbons were to rest uneasily for the next years to come.

Now that the old order of his world was being threatened, Goya was discovering new tensions within himself. Ever since he was first made a member of the Academy he had known his colleague Gaspar Melchor de Jovellanos (1774–1811), the most prominent and brilliant liberal thinker and writer of his day in Spain. Jovellanos had got Goya the commission for the paintings at Salamanca, and had probably put many another job in his way. Goya listened to and believed in the ideas and ideals of this man of genius and sensitivity—statesman, collector, poet, and dramatist, whose 1787 treatise on the agricultural laws of Spain was to be the charter of Spanish liberalism.

A disciple of the French *Encyclopédistes,* and the translator into Spanish of Rousseau's *Social Contract,* Jovellanos was dedicated to restoring his country to the position of eminence in politics and literature which it had enjoyed during the Golden Age of the sixteenth century. Many schemes for this regeneration are outlined in the open letters Jovellanos exchanged with Cabarrus.

Jovellanos' was not a lone voice. Over three hundred sets of the *Encyclopédie,* that compendium of rational thinking, had been subscribed to in Spain. It was being pored over by such liberal-minded friends of Goya as François Cabarrus and Ceán Bermúdez, the critic and art historian. When he was the Chief Clerk in the office of the Secretary of the Bank of San Carlos, Ceán Bermúdez had persuaded Goya to invest in the bank, and had procured him the commissions for portraits of its directors.

Jovellanos believed that society should be improved from above and within the established order, a position different from that of the revolutionaries who soon were to create a reign of terror in France. Everyone in public life, he thought, was obliged to seek the happiness of individuals, of country, of mankind. The method was through education. Thus private morality would lead to public morality, and both would procure prosperity.

That Goya adopted Jovellanos' liberal theories is indi-

Gaspar Melchor de Jovellanos. *Collection of Visconde de Irueste, Madrid.*

PHOTO MAS, BARCELONA

cated by his support of the educational principles of the Swiss educational reformer Johann Heinrich Pestalozzi (1746-1827). When a Pestalozzi school was opened in Madrid in 1806,[1] Goya donated the sign he painted for it, and also designed the title page of Pestalozzi's *ABC of Sense Impressions*. Like Jovellanos, Pestalozzi believed that individual and social reform could come only through the moral and intellectual improvement of the individual by means of educational effort. Goya also quoted Jovellanos' satires in the captions of the *Caprichos*.

At the time of the accession of Charles IV, Goya was standing on the threshold of a new way of life and thought. His paintings in the previous few years, with their satire and irony and their themes of work, show that he was already finding how new, reshaping forces were making obsolete the old patterns of behavior. He was beginning to look toward a day when people would meet and love one another as human beings, not as noble and commoner. His conscience was becoming that of the modern man.

There was forming in his mind a new philosophy that the end and aim of life was man's freedom to live by Truth. In this sense, Truth meant to Goya man's natural reason —his true nature—and that definition was in his thought when he said that his three masters were nature, Velázquez, and Rembrandt. Like most of his contemporaries, Goya had small interest in nature as expressed in trees, mountains, rivers, rocks, and so forth. Only two of his paintings make any statement whatever about landscape. Man was his concern. He began to depict the common people in the ancient struggle of man to attain Truth by and for himself. Man's efforts for Truth and Freedom, Goya thought, were the essential for human happiness.

[1] The school was under the patronage of the then prime minister, Manuel Godoy, who pretended an interest in education. Godoy was a powerful patron of Goya. The situation is typical of the difficulty encountered in trying to separate Goya's sincere beliefs from his opportunism.

King Charles IV of Spain. *Capodimonte Museum, Naples.*

Queen Maria Luisa of Spain. *Capodimonte Museum, Naples.*

These incubating ideas were naturally in conflict with those of the depraved Court, to whose charmed circle Goya had just been admitted. There the only enlightenment was the rebellious Maria Luisa's cynical contempt for convention.

For the time being, Goya decided to go along with the attitudes of that circle. By February 20, 1790, the king and queen had sat to him for the first of the many official portraits he would paint of them. These were intended as a gift to Charles IV's brother, the king of Naples, and now hang in the Capodimonte Museum in Naples.

Of all the royalty he painted, these two members fared the best at Goya's hand. He seems to have liked them, probably because they appeared to like him and had honored him. Charles talked to Goya about agricultural problems in Aragon, Goya's life there, Goya's personal affairs. The king even embraced him.

Still, for all this rapport between them, Goya's eye was too honest to disguise what he saw in the king. Perhaps unconsciously Goya showed the man's shortcomings. The king was a physically powerful man who practiced boxing, loved open-air exercise and hunting, and had a gargantuan appetite. These pursuits kept him from cultivating what little intellect he had, and may have made him asthmatic as well. All these qualities appear in the portrait, along with smugness. Nevertheless, Charles seems likable, almost pathetically so. And the pose, derived from Velázquez' grand manner, makes him infinitely royal in spite of his favorite hunting costume.

Maria Luisa, in a gorgeous yellow gown, and sparkling with jewels, is also every inch a queen—and every inch a harpy. Goya leaves nothing unsaid of both sides of her character. They seem to have fascinated him; certainly he was not bored with her, for the portrait is almost too alive for comfort. In it Goya made a statement about human nature—about a forceful human being—without qualifying it with a moral judgment.

By this time Goya had grown sufficiently experienced to be tolerant. The portrait of Maria Luisa is a mature, sophisticated interpretation of a woman not afraid to play for high stakes and who won by showing no mercy to her opponents. If history has decided that Maria Luisa played her cards none too well and cheated a little during the game, Goya was in no position to take that long perspective. He preferred to accept the challenge and play along with her. He could see clearly, but he was not clairvoyant.

Maria Luisa could see clearly too. She recognized that Goya was telling the truth about her for posterity. She was brave enough to let it stand. She ordered at least ten other portraits from him.

Goya's peasant heart was bursting with pride. The king had actually played the violin for him! He even felt secure enough financially to write Zapater in May, 1790, asking Martín to see that Goya's mother had all the money she needed. He betrayed himself, however, by adding that he hoped his brothers could look after themselves. Always basically naïve, he made it clear that his generosity was less charity than self-advancement. He would paint a portrait without charge if he thought it would be to his advantage, but he did not wish to be importuned by persons from whom he could expect nothing in return.

Basking in the friendship of his sovereigns, Goya began to take liberties at Court. Once he arrived in white stockings. When a majordomo informed him that these were not suitable attire, Goya drew caricatures all over them of the Court sycophants and petty officials, including even the crown prince's chaplain and adviser, Juan Escóiquiz. Then he paraded up the grand staircase of the palace so that everyone could see the fun.

His fame had spread to the provinces. In August of the

same year he went to Valencia with Josefa, whose doctors had recommended sea air for her convalescence from some illness she had suffered during the summer. His fellow painters gave a lavish reception for him in that seacoast city, and the Academy of San Carlos there made him an honorary member in return for two drawings he presented to it. He painted the Archbishop of Valencia. While Josefa rested, he hunted in the nearby marshes of Altufera.

The new honors were not without their compensations. Goya thought he should lead a life to match his dignified position. He sent Zapater some popular music, commenting a little ruefully that he himself no longer should go to the places where he could hear it. Once Goya had written his friend that in the short time given him on earth, every man should live as he wished. Now it was not so much what life Goya wanted as what life would most profit him. It was more fitting for him now to be seen at the *tertulias* of the Duchess of Osuna than at bullfights and in the taverns of the Lavapié. He could improve his mind at these intellectual parties, and meet and come to know influential persons. But he never lost his love for the music of the people.

In October he was back in Zaragoza, probably having been summoned by Don Ramón Pignatelli. This philanthropist had founded an institution there to help the unemployed, not by alms but by finding work for them in the local industries he wanted developed. A member of the Fuentes family, who had first recognized Goya's potentialities, Don Ramón had also brought to completion the Aragon Canal, begun two hundred years before.

Goya reveled in the deference paid him by the great ones of a city that a scant ten years before had as good as thrown him out. Among them was Don Juan Martín de Goicoechea, a lover and patron of the arts, who had founded a

Martin Zapater. *Collection Durand-Ruel, Paris.*
PHOTO MAS, BARCELONA

high school of art and maintained it for eight years at his own expense. Later it became the Academy of San Luis. Like Jovellanos, the philanthropic Goicoechea was a patriotic liberal who earnestly worked for the restoration of his country's prestige. Later, Goya's son Javier would marry the daughter of this locally important man and of his wife, Doña Juana de Galarza.

Goya also reveled in being together again with Martín Zapater. As a labor of love and token of affection he painted a portrait of his old friend, inscribing it: "done with all the skill I have." When they parted, Goya promised to come back soon. A year later, he spent two months with Martín in Zaragoza, hunting and otherwise relaxing for a much needed vacation.

For when Goya had returned to Madrid in the late autumn of 1790, he was tired and in poor health. He decided to do nothing he did not want to do, paint no one who did not excite him. He was developing a new approach to portraiture, trying to get away from the bright colors the Italian and French painters had made conventional. He was tired of painting purely for decorative effect. He wanted to depict the truth—the essence—of what he saw, not a mere imitation. He was arriving at a conception of art not unlike the definition his contemporary, William Wordsworth, would soon give it: "a known and familiar landscape over which is thrown a certain coloring of the imagination that constitutes poetic truth."

In his portrait of the Duke of Osuna (page 93) Goya had already tried to draw without lines; that is, to construct forms, not fill in outlines. Here, too, he was trying to paint without making a painting—to reproduce not things but the sensations he felt about things and their relation to time and space.

This new way of looking at objects led to a change in the tones of Goya's palette. He was beginning his "gray" period, in which grays, silvery blues, carmine, and violet would replace the reds and yellows and greens he had favored because they were fashionable. He still kept his beloved vermilion to bring out these muted tones and give a true value to each gray. Eventually the vermilion would soften to rose.

At this time of experiment toward progress, Goya was forced to return to the tapestry cartoons he had agreed to complete. By April, 1791, the director of the factory, Livinio Stuiks, resolved to report to the Minister of Finance that because the painters were slacking off, his workmen had to be laid off. Stuiks signaled out Goya for especial blame because Goya had claimed that his appointment as Court Painter freed him from obligation to the factory. Goya, Stuiks claimed, was "absolutely without occupation," whereas Ramón Bayeu, another dilatory designer, was truly engaged in more urgent work.

Goya remained obstinate. Stuiks persuaded the Minister of Finance, whose jurisdiction included the tapestry manufacture, to intervene personally. Goya was on the verge of official disgrace when Francisco Bayeu stepped into the dispute. Bayeu, who was then Director of the Academy, used his influence as Goya's superior there, and also as a brother-in-law careful of his sister's welfare, to make Goya see that his stubborn vanity could well ruin the entire family.

Goya relented. The feud with Bayeu was patched up. Goya wrote him on June 3, 1791: "I am very sorry that our relations should have been disturbed. I pray God to take away my pride, which rules me on occasions like these. I will try to control myself and not to fly into a rage again so that my actions will be less evil during the rest of my life."

Gossiping Women. *Courtesy of the Wadsworth Atheneum, Hartford.*

it was intended for hanging over a doorway, perhaps in the king's study in the Escorial. Goya made a brilliant use of two reclining figures to fit this awkwardly narrow space.

It is a good example of the humor Goya instilled into the scenes of the cartoons. The two *majas* are at the same time individuals and types of all women since time began, trading tidbits of human interest in the neighborhood over the back fence. The gesture of the woman facing outward, her arms akimbo, practically speaks her indignation at the "secret" her friend is, through an equally eloquent gesture, "confiding."

The summer of 1792, when Goya was finishing the tapestry cartoons, brought disturbing news from France. Already the progress of the Revolution there had caused Floridablanca to put an embargo on all things French, lest ideas from France cross the Pyrenees and inspire the Spanish people to do to their Bourbons what the French were doing to theirs. Although Floridablanca had once belonged to the Spanish intellectual movement, he now thought it wise to abandon it. All revolutionary literature was suppressed in Spain; so were the newspapers, except for the official *Diario de Madrid;* so were the chairs of political science in the universities.

At Court any sympathizer with these proscribed doctrines was highly suspect. Jovellanos and Cabarrus were exiled. Even Floridablanca was forced out of office through a palace intrigue, and the Count of Aranda was recalled to ensure the safety of the French Bourbon King Louis XVI, Charles IV's cousin. After news of the attack on the Tuileries, on June 20, and the imprisonment of Louis in September, the fears of the Spanish Court for its own safety reached panic proportions. Charles IV had never forgotten the Madrid mob of 1767. He dreaded the power of the common people.

Goya was in a panic for different reasons. His association with Jovellanos and Cabarrus and with the liberals in both Madrid and Zaragoza were well known. Floridablanca, who might have protected him, was in peril himself. Goya could not bear the thought that everything he had worked so hard to attain and which he had enjoyed for so short a time should suddenly be snatched from him. He decided to get out of town while the getting was good.

In Cádiz, far to the south, he had a friend in Sebastián Martínez y Pérez, Treasurer General of the Council of Finances and member of the Royal Council of the Public Treasury. Martínez was less than five months older than Goya, and a lover of art. In his house on the Calle de Bilbao he had a collection of three hundred paintings, and a library of books and prints.

Goya arrived there in the fall of 1792—after September 2, when he attended a meeting of the Academy of San Fernando—and immediately showed his gratitude for this asylum by painting Martínez' portrait, which is now in the Metropolitan Museum of Art, New York City. One of Goya's best works, it is painted in the new tones he was trying, even though it is still much in the French manner.

Goya stayed two months in the dazzling blue-and-white seaport city of Cádiz, whose trade made it far from provincial. The merchants and the local nobility had imported works of art from England, France, and other countries. In their palaces Goya might easily have seen works of many artists with whom he was not familiar. It is possible that in Cádiz he encountered some portraits by Gainsborough and Raeburn, elements of whose style he later adopted.

Then, apparently to visit the ancient capital of Seville, Goya went on a tour. He fell sick.

The immediate cause may have been a fever brought on by Goya's overheating himself while repairing the axle of

He expressed his thanks to his brother-in-law, and showed his willingness to make amends by sending Bayeu the sketch for a cartoon.

For the next year Goya kept to his good intentions and finished the cartoons he had promised. But he had little interest in this work, which, owing to its decorative nature, kept him from pursuing his new theories about painting.

One of the best of these last cartoons is the *Gossiping Women* in the Wadsworth Atheneum, Hartford, Connecticut. Its shape indicates that the tapestry to be woven from the coach in which he was excursioning. The story goes that he built a fire in the cold night air, and over it forged the broken shaft with his own powerful hands. This, however, is probably only one of the many legends about him.

At any rate, he wrote to the Academy in January, 1793, asking for a vacation from his duties there in order to mend his health. By March 19, 1793, he was back at Martínez' house under the care of a doctor.

It is now impossible to determine the exact nature of the disease that smote Goya. A letter of Martínez describes it as "entirely in his head," and recent research indicates that it was a kind of paralysis of the nerves. Possibly it had been brought on by Goya's nervous tension and overwork during the previous three years. It seems to have been largely of psychosomatic origin. Or it may have been due ultimately to the aural disorders he had had since childhood.

Medical science in Spain in the eighteenth century was practically nonexistent. Medical practice was barbarous and primitive, consisting mostly of bleeding and purges. That Goya recovered at all was due wholly to his rugged physique. The illness was so terrible, according to Zapater, that the artist's future was despaired of. It left Goya absolutely deaf.

It also changed his personality. Thirty-five years remained to him, but throughout them he was a different man.

7

A New Vision

By July, 1793, Goya had recovered sufficiently to return to his home in Madrid. But he was far from well. His disease, most recently described as neurolabyrinthitis and as a Vogt-Koyanagi syndrome, had so paralyzed a group of his muscles that for a year and a half he could not control a pen sufficiently to write a letter. For the rest of his life he was to be troubled with dizziness, blurred vision, and a fearful ringing in his now-deaf ears.

The deafness isolated Goya from much of the society he had known. It threw him back upon himself, making him dependent for inspiration on his inner resources of memory and imagination. Had Goya not been such an extrovert, the affliction might not have affected his psychology so markedly. Descending on him as it did at the height of his worldly success, it struck him as a blow from an unkind fate. He bitterly resented it, for he could not understand why he had deserved it. His nature, which had shown traces of paranoia, now began to exhibit a mild schizophrenia.

The result was that Goya constructed a world of his own. Because his simple faith made God the author and cause of all events, he could see in this judgment upon him only the hostility of the Almighty. He was an outcast in an inimical world. What guilt he felt he transferred to the Deity.

The exuberant optimism of his letters to Zapater, the high hopes he had for always the immediate future, changed to pessimism, loneliness, despair. On April 23, 1794, he wrote his friend: "Sometimes I am so disturbed in mind that I cannot bear myself. At other times I am calm, as now when I am writing you. But I am always tired. Next Monday, if God permit, I will go to a bullfight. I wish you were here to go with me."

It was a terrible mental effort for him to reconstruct his world. If he were to go on living, he had to find a new way of life. Rebelliousness against interference with his ego by persons he despised changed to revolt against the very hand of God. This revolt took the form of an assertion of a new world in which Goya himself would triumph. The only means he had was his art.

If his illness had not produced this need for assertion, Goya might have finished his existence as little more than a competent painter whose artistic vision ranged not far beyond that of the fashionable conventions of his day. He had been too content with quick and easy recognition, with money and celebrity, to think of enduring fame and the distant future. He had gratified his ego rather than striven to complete himself by fulfilling all his potentialities. He had put the pursuit of pleasure before the pursuit of happiness.

Now he was forced to be a creative genius. So great had become the tensions of his complex of emotions that they could now be expressed forcefully. He was no longer to reproduce what he saw, but would transform it.

His new vision of the world would release the tensions of others so that they could see meanings in life veiled from them by their own too intense involvement in it. Removed above this preoccupation with daily living by his deafness and spiritual isolation, Goya could see the particulars of existence in perspective; that is, in relationship to one another and to himself. The will to surmount the hostility of fate elevated Goya above the plane of his infirmity.

Points on a plane are isolated, invisible behind one another. If Point A on a plane represents the Past; Point B, the Present; and Point C, the Future; then a person on the same plane at Point B can see only one at a time. His perception is inadequate. All three points must be seen together in relationship to one another.

An intelligent human being quickly senses that inadequacy. It hinders his progress, his perfecting or completing of himself. A conflict occurs. The force of the conflict raises him, as it were, in proportion to the power of his will to perfect himself, to a level from which he sees all three points at once. The higher his will propels him, the more of Point A and of Point C he can explore. Combining all three gives him a vision of time and space. This he can transmit to less elevated minds. They, then, rise a certain part of the way toward understanding.

Such is the function of the true artist. It is his obligation both to himself and to the society that supports him. This is what Goya's will to survive produced in him.

The paintings, engravings, and drawings Goya created after his illness show his reaction to it. It enriched his art by requiring him to rely on himself. His art transformed his illness from a defeat to a victory. His illness had given him new mental experiences. Out of these his art built a new world. Goya's personality coordinated the two; that is, the world of others and his own. His personality acts as a guide for others to the meanings of Goya's own world. After exploring that, others can better understand their own. Goya's art thus becomes, as he would call it, "the universal idiom."

Goya's determination to rescue himself from the physical and spiritual morass of his affliction drove him to take up his brush even before he could handle a pen. He had new thoughts to express, new visions to record. By the end of 1793 he had painted his manifestos of a new dimension in art.

On January 4, 1794, Goya wrote to his friend Bernardo de Iriarte, Vice-Protector of the Academy of San Fernando: "To occupy my imagination, which has been tormented by the thought of my ailments, and to cover part of the great expense they have caused me, I have been painting a number of easel pictures. They have given me a chance to make observations that commissioned works do not allow me. I have found room in these to expand fantasy and imagination."

The Academy acknowledged receipt of eleven paintings from Goya, saying that the "organization took much pleasure in seeing them, praising their merit and Goya's own." It was a relief to Goya to find that the canvases met with the approval of academicians, for the pictures are far from academic.

It is now impossible to say accurately which of the paintings by Goya presently in the Academy were the ones he referred to in his letter to Iriarte. Technical analyses tend to put some of them at a later date. Probably, however, *The Madhouse* was one of them.

Goya had visited the asylum for the insane on his last trip to Zaragoza. Now he was recording his impression of it. He did not wish to represent it as real, but to make it seem real by creating an illusion of madness. The difference may become clearer if the reader compares *The Madhouse* to *The Witches' Sabbath* and the other "witch" pictures Goya did for the Osuna palace of Alameda. In them he painted the fantastic and horrible as if it were real. The result approaches the ludicrous. But the illusion of *The Madhouse* transmits the terror of tragedy.

It is not that Goya had seen his subject matter with dif-

The Madhouse. *Academy of San Fernando, Madrid.*

ferent eyes so much as that he had learned how to transform what he saw. He adopted a technique that affects the
eye of the spectator so as to produce in him the emotional
response Goya desires. Goya had explored human psychology sufficiently to understand that emotions are the result
of impressions received through the senses.

Goya's choice of subject matter may puzzle persons who
think that art should treat only those aspects of life which
are immediately pleasing to the senses: handsome people,
harmonious landscapes, animals whose actions are made
to resemble those of human beings, flowers, noble deeds.
This attitude is a misconception of the "beautiful" and of
the function of art.

136

To the genuine artist all aspects of life are important. He recognizes that the "beautiful" is the exception; the "ugly" is the rule. He strives to integrate the two. Insanity, Goya says in *The Madhouse,* must be understood if sanity is to be. Horror must be transformed into pity. The afflicted are as much a part of truth as the whole; the deaf man as important as the man of flawless hearing. Life is best revealed by its brinks. The comedy of day merges imperceptibly with the tragedy of night. Each is "beautiful" because neither can exist without the other.

If, for the sake of argument, *The Madhouse,* undated though it is, can be taken as the first of Goya's paintings of "fantasy and imagination," then it is Goya's breakthrough into the mind and the world of modern man. It is his shattering of the myth that Good and Evil, the beautiful and the ugly, have separate identities. With this picture Goya changes from a painter to an artist, from a chronicler to a philosopher.

The figures in *The Madhouse* are tragic because they are obscured, not highlighted. Insanity is not the subject but the predicate. It is the world beyond the immediate, a world of space yet unexplored, not understood, but ever present. Beyond the dim swarm of inmates on the left lies the darkness of the passage at the right. The figures of the man with a feathered headdress, of the fighter, of the singer, and of the mitred "Pope" are separated from the mass. They are the types of madness by which the numberless nonindividualized unfortunates can be understood. Thus Goya expresses the essence of insanity without representing it.

In *The Madhouse* there is none of the tight, defining drawing of the tapestry cartoons and the early portraits. Instead, there is Goya's expressive broken line. Shadows are accents. This is the true seeing that Goya was striving for. It permits the spectator to see for himself and to experience for himself, not as Goya would command but as Goya would direct. As Goya would later say: "Where are there lines in nature? I can see only luminous or obscure masses, planes that advance or planes that recede, reliefs or backgrounds." His whole philosophy of execution is summed up in *The Madhouse.*

Goya was through with fiction. As he became a force in painting, he abolished decoration as an end in art. The revulsion he had long felt at having to work in the Italian or the French style he now made positive. The torment he himself was experiencing found an outlet in the torment he saw in a world that had ignored realities too long. That world was being forced by the ruin it was bringing upon itself to acknowledge more than candy-box sweetness and artificiality. The French had killed their king and queen and were killing hundreds of other nonrealists daily. Maria Luisa was polluting the Spanish Court and through it her country.

This set of easel pictures marks the beginning of Goya's "black" style. The colors are dark. Light colors are used only in small, isolated patches to give power and movement. The bright splashes seem to represent Goya's conclusion that life is a painful story in which joy is but an occasional interlude.

Another example of Goya's new expressionism is *The Burial of the Sardine,* which probably belongs to the same series. This abstracts the essence of the traditional carnival of Ash Wednesday, which took place in the Pradera del Canal in Madrid. The "sardine" was originally a pig; in Goya's time it was a huge wineskin dressed as a man. A procession of monks and priests carrying a banner, bladders and figs on long poles, brooms and syringes, would conduct the "sardine" to the field. There they would march around it, chanting, and sprinkling the masked bystanders with water squirted from the syringes or shaken from the brooms. A hole was dug, and the "corpse" was laid in it. Then followed much drinking from the "corpse," feasting, and dancing.

Goya shows the mood of the carnival more than its actuality. But it is not all ribald gaiety. There is an ominous feeling in the crowd that has gathered apparently from nowhere. Individuals are lost in the dark, shapeless mass surrounding the three grotesque dancing figures in the second plane of the picture. The angular silhouette of the

The Burial of the Sardine. *Academy of San Fernando, Madrid.*

banner and the sharp shifts in the direction of the movements of the figures give the scene a strange tension. Beyond the brink of frivolity, it seems to say, lies the end of the world.

The Court of the Inquisition, another of the series, expresses Goya's disillusionment at being personally oppressed by the God he had trusted and revered. His own faith was too simple to be profound. The injustices of the Inquisition symbolize for him here the unjust "punishment" he thought had been visited upon him in the form of his deafness. Here again a sinister crowd emerges from a dark nowhere to punish without appeal. It is Goya's version of the human dilemma. Man has no direct relationship with God, only with Time and the factors of his own world.

Along with it, *The Procession of the Flagellants* expresses Goya's disgust with the superstition that through penance man may find salvation. Flagellation had actually

Procession of Flagellants. *Academy of San Fernando, Madrid.*
PHOTO MAS, BARCELONA

been abolished in Spain in 1777, but Goya and his contemporaries could vividly recall the processions during Holy Week in which ruffians would strip to the waist and flog themselves and one another with thongs tipped with glass-studded balls of wax. Their blood spattering on the bystanders was supposed to bring good health.

The picture is full of irony. Images of saints look blindly down on the penitents' travesty of worship, advertised by black-suited men with trumpets. The procession winds out of shadows toward crosses silhouetted against the sky. But that distant Calvary will expiate nothing.

The triangle of the first plane ironically recalls the triangular composition of one of Goya's most charming decorative paintings, *The Meadow of San Isidro* (now in the Prado), done only a few years earlier for the Osuna summer palace. This represents the merrymaking of the Madrileños on May 15, the feast day of their patron saint, Isidro.

The Bullfight. *The Metropolitan Museum of Art, New York, Wolfe Fund.*

Every guild and society was obliged to join the parade from the Royal Collegiate Church of San Isidro to the shrine of the saint in a meadow on the west bank of the Manzanares. The shrine marked the spot where San Isidro (1082–1170), while ploughing, had struck a spring whose waters cured the afflicted, among them Philip II. There the pleasure-bent people paid homage to the saint, drank the water of the miraculous spring by his hermitage, and picnicked.

The three-foot-by-one frame encloses a vast space: the meadow of the first plane, the innumerable picnickers of the second, the Manzanares River beyond, and, still farther off, a panorama of Madrid. All is light and gaiety, polite lovemaking, dainty dining. This was the world Goya now spurned. For years to come he would see only the black triangle, the senseless self-mortification of *The Procession of the Flagellants*.

Goya was expressing feelings now, not facts. Objects he included only to stimulate emotions. The objects themselves are not necessarily even realistic. Often they are distorted, for Goya was now saying what he had long observed and believed—that things have meaning rather than definition. And more than one meaning. The extensional form of an object is merely the beginning of its total form, which comprises all it suggests.

Thought and feeling had become more important to Goya than simple reproducing. The impression, he believed, is more informative than the depiction. Where suggestions are made to the spectator, he completes them. The spectator himself contributes to the event, becomes involved in it as his feelings respond to those of the artist. He is lured by this appeal to participate in those lines of figures, spectators themselves, which Goya was placing in the first planes of his compositions. Impressionism in art had been born.

The Meadow of San Isidro. *Prado Museum, Madrid.*

If Goya was denying the reconciliation of man with God, he was affirming the reconciliation of man with art. Artist and spectator become one in understanding. A picture was no longer to tell a story or preach a sermon, but to expand the spectator's own understanding of the world that is his context.

The Bullfight in a Small Town, which was also one of Goya's pictures given to the Academy, is a triumph of this impressionistic seeing. An enormous expanse is compressed into a very small area of canvas. Nothing is literally accurate, but everything is intensely real because of the expressiveness of Goya's broken-line—that is, impressionistic—drawing. Goya's warm feelings about the scene are so numerous and so intense that they have become blurred. They vibrate. They charge the spectator's feelings with emotional electricity.

Goya's device is to contrast spots of bright color. These he distributes over the soft grays and blacks of the masses of form. The spectator's eye, therefore, is snatched hither and yon, as in the furious activity of an actual *corrida*. Nothing is static or decorative; all is movement and reality.

Goya later preferred the more economical medium of drawing and engraving to express his feelings about his favorite sport. A later bullfight painting, however, hangs in New York City's Metropolitan Museum of Art. It is possibly in an unfinished state, yet its imprecise contours may be a deliberate invitation to the spectator to share Goya's enthusiasm for the pageantry of the bullring by completing the outlines himself. This *Bullfight* is also remarkable for the amount of space it includes within a small frame, and for the impression of excited action it gives.

The whole change in Goya's body and mind is vividly expressed in the pen-and-brush portrait (frontispiece) he made of himself about this time. It, too, is in the Metropolitan Museum. Here is no longer the cocky youth or the curled dandy or the exhibitionist showing how he worked or displaying his achievements. Here he is self-contained, brooding, peering both into himself and into the future. The once round face has grown haggard. The exuberant pride of expression is now a solemn inquisitiveness.

There is great similarity between this self-portrait and the portraits of Beethoven, Goya's younger contemporary, who would revolutionize music as Goya was altering the direction of painting. Both were stone-deaf, deaf to the demands of a world that resisted imperative changes in the means of understanding itself. Both were listening only to what each heard of the call of the future.

There would be no more of the empty-headed decorative designs for the royal tapestries. In April, 1795, Goya got a release from his obligations to the factory for reasons of health. He kept on painting, however, though not, as Bayeu reported, "with his former fervor and persistence."

Poor, hard-working, obedient, conventional Francisco

Bayeu never understood his tempestuous brother-in-law or lived to see the eventual triumph of Goya over the rules Bayeu had tried to impress upon him. On August 4, 1795, Bayeu died. Later that month Goya sent to the Academy the portrait he had made posthumously of his late brother-in-law. He wished both to honor the deceased director and, perhaps, to express his gratitude to Bayeu. He was ashamed to have quarreled so bitterly with him. The iridescent, pearl-gray painting, based on Bayeu's self-portrait, is one of Goya's finest works.

On October 4, 1795, Goya was elected to succeed Bayeu as Director of the School of Painting of the Academy of Fine Arts of San Fernando.

Not the honor or the salary of fifty doubloons (about $800) was of paramount importance to Goya. Another change in his life superseded all else. He had become involved at about this same time with the Duchess of Alba.

When this bewitching woman was baptized on June 11,

Francisco Bayeu. *Prado Museum, Madrid.*
PHOTO MAS, BARCELONA

1762, the day after her birth, she was given thirty-one Christian names. She was addressed, however, by only the first three: Maria (del Pilar) Teresa Cayetana. At the age of eight she became heiress of the ancient glory of the house of Alba and of the immense fortune—greater than that of the king—which it had accumulated over the centuries.

Her father, a disciple of Jean Jacques Rousseau, with whom he corresponded, brought her up in keeping with the educational principles of that philosopher's *Emile,* published the year she was born. No instruction was necessary for a girl, Rousseau maintained, only that she be trained to care for, advise, and console a man. Maria Teresa Cayetana interpreted this recommendation in her own way.

Her mother set her an example of emancipation from social convention. This capricious woman, Mariana de Silva y Sarmiento, Duchess of Huescar, dabbled in the arts and patronized them with that part of her passionate nature not gratified in other ways. After the death of Maria Teresa Cayetana's father, the Duchess of Huescar remarried twice. Her second husband was the aged Count of Fuentes, whose family had patronized Goya. It was probably due to this connection that Goya first became acquainted with Maria Teresa.

At the age of thirteen Goya's duchess had married the nineteen-year-old Marquis of Villafranca, and made him thereby the thirteenth Duke of Alba. He was a sickly, ineffectual man, whose chief delight was music. He commissioned compositions from Franz Joseph Haydn. One of Goya's two portraits of the duke shows him leaning on a clavichord and perusing one of Haydn's scores. He also spent much time hunting with Charles IV.

His duchess, who had retained control of a large part of

her property, was independent in many other ways, and far from ineffectual. To her enormous inheritance she added a beauty that made a French traveler in Spain, Fleurot de Langle, write of her that she had "not a hair of her head that does not provoke desire. Nothing on earth is as lovely as she. It would be impossible to surpass her. When she drives through the streets, everyone looks out the windows at her, and even the children stop their games to stare at her."

At Court she was the rival of Goya's patroness, the Duchess of Osuna. If the Duchess of Osuna declared Gluck the greatest of composers, the Duchess of Alba supported Lully. The Duchess of Osuna claimed the favors of the *torero* Pepe Hillo; the Duchess of Alba attached Costillares and Pedro Romero. The Duchess of Osuna declared that Josefa Figeras should be the new leading lady of Manuel Martínez' theatrical troupe; the Duchess of Alba saw to it that the gypsy Rosario Fernández, "La Tirana," got the position.

Queen Maria Luisa was furiously jealous of the younger, far more beautiful Maria Teresa Cayetana, who had not hesitated to steal one of the queen's lovers. The duchess taunted her by dressing the maids of the Alba household in copies of the queen's latest French gowns, and parading them in the Prado. Maria Luisa's revenge was to banish the impudent duchess from Court.

Maria Teresa Cayetana had no intention of permitting her rivals the exclusive patronage of Spain's most prominent painter. To clinch his loyalty, she presented herself at his studio with the request that he apply her makeup. She wanted her face as beautifully painted as those in Goya's portraits. Goya wrote Zapater in 1795 that the bizarre commission gave him more pleasure than painting on canvas. He added that he was to paint *"la de Alba"* at full length as soon as he finished the work he had in hand.

This was the beginning of the relationship between the Duchess of Alba and Goya which has puzzled many biographers. The truth of the matter can only be inferred. The duchess was no letter writer, and Goya wrote almost nothing about her to Martín Zapater.

The evidence is that Goya painted the Duchess of Alba as least three times before the year 1795 was out. The full-length portrait he mentioned to Zapater, still in the collection of the Duke of Alba in Madrid's Liria Palace, is not entirely successful. She seems imperious but immature. Goya had not yet got far into her character.

Two small paintings, also dated 1795, show the duchess in less formal poses. In one she is in a fit of temper, attacking her old duenna, Rafaela Luisa Velázquez, whom in less fiery moments she called *La Beata* (The Blessed One). In the other she is with her two "adopted" children: the little Negress Maria de la Luz, whom she had picked up on a roadside; and Luis, the four- or five-year-old son of her majordomo Tomás de Berganza. For though the duchess was childless, she had maternal feelings.

Later Goya drew her hysterical over the imminent death of her little woolly white dog, and showed himself trying to resuscitate it. By then, Goya understood at least two extremes of her character.'

The duchess sent Josefa Goya elegant delicacies from the kitchen of the palace on Alba Street, in Madrid's gypsy quarter. Josefa was expected to keep the gold and silver dishes in which they arrived. Goya probably interpreted this generous attention as no more personally intended than the infanta's gift of an elegant gown to his wife. He could have been interested in Maria Teresa Cayetana only as a model who would have delighted any painter. The patronage of the great House of Alba was a bright feather in his professional cap. Opportunist and snob that he was, Goya enjoyed the Duchess of Alba's lavish entertainments. In her palace he could feast his artist's eyes on Raphael's magnificent *Madonna,* now in the National Gallery, Washington, D. C.; and on Velázquez' gorgeous nude *Venus with a Looking Glass* (the "Rokeby Venus"), now in London's National Gallery.

The Duke of Alba died in Seville on June 9, 1796. The duchess retired for her period of hardly sincere mourning to her palace at nearby Sanlúcar de Barrameda.

Goya left Madrid on October 2 of that year. He did not return until the following April 1. Two albums of drawings, many of which are scenes of the duchess' household, make it clear that for most of those six months he was with her at Sanlúcar.

The Duchess of Alba was thirty-four years old, and beautiful. Goya turned fifty before he was back in Madrid. He was deaf, ugly, and often disagreeable. That there was a violent love affair between them, as the romantic version of the relationship would have it, seems, in the circumstances, unlikely. The duchess could have had any lover she wanted. Goya was too experienced in the wiles of the women of the Spanish Court to be misled into thinking that Maria Teresa Cayetana's flirtations were serious. For at least three years his mind had been occupied with designing the series of satirical etchings he would call the *Caprichos.* Several of these are based on the drawings he made at Sanlúcar. This is an indication that mature, bitter, almost cynical Goya saw in the young, giddy duchess the same corruption he was seeing in the whole degenerate society he had once coveted.

On the other hand, many of the Sanlúcar drawings are gay and full of humor, as if to say that Goya enjoyed himself there. Others show that he appreciated the voluptuous-ness of the duchess. While he was with her he saw to it that she included a pension of the equivalent of about $250 a year for Javier Goya in the will she signed in February, 1797. And he kept for himself the second and great full-length portrait of her he painted in 1797.

This now hangs in the Hispanic Society of America, New York City. The duchess is in the costume Spanish women wore out of doors in the country—a black mantilla and *basquiña*. About her waist is a red sash with gold fringe. The gold cloth of her bodice gleams through the black lace of the mantilla. A white and yellow bow accents her black hair. The dexterity of Goya's technique is nothing short of marvelous.

A tempting clue to the relationship between painter and model is the two rings the duchess wears on her right hand, one inscribed "Alba"; the other, "Goya." And with her right index finger she points to an inscription on the sand. This reads "Solo Goya" facing the duchess, and "1797" facing the spectator.

The "solo" can be interpreted as simply "unaided," in which case it appears as a kind of private joke like "without any help from his parents or teacher." Or it can mean "yours alone."

Goya signed his name on at least one other ring, that worn by Doña Narcisa Barañana de Goicoechea in his portrait of her, done about 1805, and now in New York's Metropolitan Museum of Art. There has never been any hint of a romantic attachment between Goya and this kinswoman by marriage. He also inscribed his name in the sand at the feet of the Marquis of Bondad Real.

Goya may have kept the portrait because it is so consummate a piece of painting. Perhaps he wished always to remember the duchess as he knew her at Sanlúcar. Perhaps, out of spite, he would not let her have it after their parting, which seems to have been unhappy.

The Duchess of Alba. *Courtesy of the Hispanic Society of America, New York.*

The customs of high society at the time should not be overlooked in forming an opinion of the nature of the relationship between Goya and the Duchess of Alba. The institution of the *cortejo* could explain that they were merely mutually diverting companions. The duchess was bored in the country. Goya was always ready to accept an invitation to visit his rich and aristocratic patrons. The lives of neither of the two seem to have been shattered by the experience. They were too sophisticated, each in his own way, to have been the great lovers romantic writers would like to make them.

It is not clear how much Goya saw of the duchess after his visit to Sanlúcar. Apparently she bought from him his famous nudes, *The Naked Maja* and *The Clothed Maja*, for Manuel Godoy later acquired them from her estate, along with Velázquez' *Venus with a Looking Glass*.

The Duchess of Alba died on July 23, 1802, possibly having been poisoned by the jealous Queen Maria Luisa. Goya made a drawing for a mausoleum for her, but the monument was never executed. Probably he kept the sketch secret as his private reflection on his association with the duchess. The design for the tomb is significantly similar to Plate 8 of the *Caprichos*, whose caption reads: "A woman who cannot take care of herself belongs to the first man who grabs her. When it is too late, she is surprised that she has been seduced."

Goya was not at Sanlúcar all the time he was absent from Madrid. He stopped in nearby Cádiz to paint a strange *Last Supper* for the Church of Santa Cueva there. Influenced by Poussin, it is full of violent movement. Christ's prediction that He will be betrayed has caused the disciples to fall to the floor in shock. And Goya seems to have returned to Madrid via Zaragoza, where he painted another portrait of Zapater, now lost. All in all, the fabled romance with the Duchess of Alba could not have lasted more than four months.

As soon as he returned to the capital, Goya asked to be relieved of his duties as Director of the Academy of San Fernando, on grounds of health and of his deafness. The Academy expressed its profound regret, mentioning that he heard "absolutely nothing, not even the loudest noises." Communication with him had to be by writing or by sign language. The Academy accepted the resignation, and made Goya "Honorary Director."

Probably he wished to be relieved of his duties in order to have more time for completing his private project of the *Caprichos*. Isolated proofs of the etchings in this series had been pulled as early as 1796. The subjects and their execution were uppermost in Goya's mind.

He could not, however, exclude his work as Court Painter, and he had no wish to turn down a commission for three allegorical medallions—Science, Industry, Agriculture—for the splendid palace Manuel Godoy was building to house his royal bride. It is now the Ministry of the Marine in Madrid.

Godoy (1767–1851) was then the most powerful man in Spain. Even the king deferred to him and honored him. Son of a noble but impoverished family of Badajoz, a town near the Portuguese border, he had become, at the age of seventeen, one of the king's bodyguard. In that capacity he caught the eye of Queen Maria Luisa, and became the fifth of her known string of lovers. (She was to have two more after Godoy, and probably had others as well.) He followed his brother Luis, who was not so patient, so lazy, and so opportunistic. Whatever else may be said of Manuel Godoy, he was good to his mother; as soon as he was installed in the royal apartments, he got her a job as lady-in-waiting to the queen.

Godoy soon rose from a humble but handsome guards-
man to be a lieutenant general and a grandee of Spain with
the title of Duke of Alcudia. In 1791, he managed to get
Floridablanca, who hated him for his influence over the
sovereigns, dismissed, and had himself appointed prime
minister. The next year, having failed to save Louis XVI
from the guillotine, Godoy declared war on the French
Republic.

The Spanish army was no match for the French one,
which was so inspired by the ideals of the Revolution—
Liberty, Equality, Brotherhood—that it actually infected
its enemies with them. As this propaganda spread, popular
opinion and threats on his life forced Godoy to negotiate
the Treaty of Basel in 1795. It won Spain nothing, but
it cost the country its portion of Santo Domingo. In spite
of the fiasco, Charles IV named Godoy "Prince of the
Peace."

Godoy became the absolute dictator of Spain. His power
in his own country led him to believe he should be a power
in international politics. In 1796 he allied Spain with
France, and declared war on England. The next year the
English fleet almost annihilated the Spanish navy, and
blockaded Spain's vital port of Cádiz. The war accumulated disasters for Spain that were climaxed in the crushing
defeat at Trafalgar on October 21, 1805.

None of these results of Godoy's intemperate policies
and headstrong domination could shake the devotion of
Maria Luisa to her fickle favorite, or Charles IV's unseeing
trust in him. To gratify Godoy's wish for a royal bride, the
sovereigns handed him Charles's seventeen-year-old cousin,
Maria Teresa de Borbón y Vallabriga, whose portrait Goya
had painted (page 83) when she was two years old. He
married her in 1797, installed her in the million-dollar
palace he had built, and made her the unhappiest woman
in the Court.

Godoy now joined Goya's list of distinguished patrons. The allegorical paintings Goya did for Godoy are far from his best work, and they were not harmonious with the elaborate decoration of the new palace. Through them, however, Goya got to know the opportunist who was preparing Spain for ruin. Godoy, who posed as a patron of education and the arts, cultivated Goya's society and treated him as an equal. It was all grist for Goya's satirical mill, which was slowly grinding out the etched plates he would gather into the *Caprichos*.

Society had changed in Madrid. The atrocities of the French Revolution, culminating in the beheading of Charles IV's royal cousin, made the formerly favored French fashions decidedly unfashionable. There was a great and sudden fondness for things Spanish. Women discarded their French furbelows and adopted the national dress of the *majas*. "Majaism," a further travesty of integrity, became the new style. But the ideas that had led to the French Revolution and its ideals were far from dead in Spain. They throve there among the intellectuals who, before they were proscribed by Floridablanca, had worked for the rehabilitation of the Spain they now saw Godoy leading to ruin.

Godoy posed as an enlightened intellectual. Consequently, he recalled Jovellanos from exile in his native Gijón, in Asturias, where he had spent his seven years of banishment working for the educational and social welfare of his province. Again in favor, Jovellanos was made Minister of Justice. Goya and he renewed their old friendship and interchange of liberal ideas.

Through Jovellanos, Goya met the erudite poet Juan Antonio Meléndez Valdés (1754–1817) who had just been made a magistrate and transferred from Castile to Madrid. Meléndez Valdés, a gentle, peace-loving man, dedicated his 1797 volume of poems to Godoy. They in-

cluded an "Ode on Fanaticism" denouncing the barbarous
auto-da-fés and urging their abolition. Goya painted his
portrait that year, and also one of Bernardo de Iriarte, the
collector and patron of literature who had just been made
Minister of Agriculture. Early the following year Goya
painted Jovellanos himself, and Francisco de Saavedra, the
new Minister of Finance and another liberal. All these
men shared their liberal ideas with one another in a kind
of intellectual underground.

Also in the group was Ferdinand Guillemardet, ambassador of the French Directorate to Spain. He arrived in
Madrid in 1798 for a brief stay before he was recalled by
Napoleon. Guillemardet had been a village doctor before
he entered politics after the fall of the Bastille in 1789. He
had voted for the execution of Louis XVI, but had later
helped put the terrorists out of power. Then he became
a partisan of the Directorate, which appointed him ambassador. He died insane in 1808.

Goya must have appreciated Guillemardet—after all,
both were of peasant origin—for he made one of his most
spectacular portraits of the ambassador. Goya departed
here from the pearly-gray tones he had been using, and
posed Guillemardet rather theatrically in a gilded chair

Ferdinand Guillemardet. *The Louvre, Paris.*

beside a table covered with yellow brocade. The cockade in the ambassador's hat, and the sash of his dark blue uniform reproduced the red, white, and blue of the French national colors. His gold sword hilt flashes light. The background is golden-green. Guillemardet himself looks at the spectator with the audacity of a true defender of the peoples' liberties. The painting glitters with the golden ideals of freedom and democracy.

By 1798 Goya seems to have deserted, if not forgotten, the Duchess of Alba. He was, at any rate, still in the good graces of her rival, the Duchess of Osuna. In that year he painted the witch scenes for the Alameda (page 95). But the great work of the year was the frescoing of the Church of San Antonio de la Florida.

La Florida was a retreat for the Madrileños from the confinement of the city—an expanse of woodlands and gardens. From time immemorial they had flocked there in the summertime, especially on June 13, the day of St. Anthony of Padua, who had been born in Lisbon in 1195, and so was considered an Iberian. He was the patron of Spanish girls of marriageable age, who would petition him for a fiancé.

Lying northwest of the royal palace and just beyond the San Vicente Gate, the area of La Florida, on the banks of the Manzanares, needed a new church. On April 22, 1792, work was begun on one by Felipe Fontana, an Italian architect imported by Charles IV to continue the beautification of the city his father had begun. Fontana was also a painter and a designer of stage settings for the theater of Buen Retiro.

The church was now ready for decoration. It is a small, well-proportioned, neoclassical building in the form of a Greek cross, with an apse. Over the crossing—the juncture of the arms of the cross—Fontana built a cupola resting on pendentives and topped by a lantern. The interior of this small dome, barely nineteen feet in diameter, Goya chose for his work. He had probably got the commission through Jovellanos sometime between the end of March and the middle of June, 1798.

For his subject matter Goya chose an incident in the life of the saint that he found in Croiset's *Christian Year,* which had recently been translated into Spanish by Father José Francisco Isla. The saint's father, Don Martin Bulloes, of a good Portuguese family, had been accused of causing a neighbor's death. Hearing of this charge, Anthony miraculously transported himself from Padua to Lisbon. After he had listened to the evidence, he could not consider his father guilty. He proposed to the avenging mob that he command the earth to give up its dead so that the murdered man could reveal the true assassin. The corpse arose and cleared the saint's father.

What must have affected Goya in this simple story is its popular appeal. As a child in Fuendetodos he had probably heard many similar miracles told the villagers by the parish priest. Lacking any mystical element, it struck him as a narrative he could illustrate without having to invent some visible symbol for an abstraction he did not grasp, like the veneration of the holy name of God.

Daringly he decided to state it in terms of the people of his own Madrid—the people of the Court, of the parks, of the streets in all sections, old and young, male and female, snaggle-toothed villains and mischievous boys. He grouped the hundred of them behind a railing, some leaning upon it, others scrambling over it—all before a sketchy landscape.

The saint himself is a simple Franciscan, hardly differentiated from the others in the crowd by his halo and the flood of light around the scene of the miracle. Not everyone is watching the miracle: some are gossiping, others are

Murals in San Antonio de la Florida.

The Miracle of St. Anthony. *San Antonio de la Florida, Madrid.*

plying their trade; one man, possibly the real murderer, is trying to break through the mob to safety. The tone is purely secular, full of the humor of humanity, almost ribald. The gorgeous colors—whites, ochers, warm greens, rose, gray-blue, lavender—are sensual rather than sacred. Flecks of vermilion and gold make the figures, all of whom are caught in a moment of suspended motion, vibrate with life.

Goya also decorated the trumpet arch of the main chapel with a triangular fresco of angels and cherubim lifting red curtains to reveal the Trinity. The angels are distinctly feminine and robustly healthy, charming heavenly chorines. Their iridescent wings, vividly lighted from below, as if by footlights, add to the luminosity of the chapel.

The work is done in true fresco style; that is, the colors were applied to wet plaster so as to dry with it. Only the vermilion is added after (*a secco*). It is lively brushwork, not daubed on with sponges, as some critics have thought because Goya ordered one and three-quarters pounds of sponges; he used these to clean up with. Goya began the actual painting on August 1, 1798. On that day the carriage stipulated in his contract arrived at his house, No. 1, Calle del Desengaño, to carry him the three-odd miles to the church and back, at a cost of about three dollars the round trip. He finished the painting by December 20, in the amazingly short time of 120 working days. Perhaps the painter Ascensio Julia assisted him.

The work is one of Goya's greatest masterpieces, and one of the world's greatest mural paintings. When Goya wrote to Zapater that all Madrid was in ecstasies about the frescoes, for once he was not exaggerating.

Later that year Goya dashed off a *Betrayal of Christ* for the Cathedral of Toledo, and exhibited it at the Academy on January 1, 1799. The figure of Christ is spotlighted in the center of a group of ruffians almost lost in the dark shadows of the Garden of Gethsemane. The Savior's expression catches His sense of having known from the beginning of time that what was happening would occur at just that moment. His figure represents His passive acceptance of it, yet also shows His human disillusionment. The whole picture is rich and somber in coloring.

Again Goya used the people of his own experience for the personages of this drama. The soldiers are reminiscent of the hideously realistic common folk of the sixteenth-century Flemish painters Hieronymus Bosch and Pieter Brueghel. Brueghel's lusty scenes of peasant life express the independent spirit of a people who sacrificed all advantages to throw off the Spanish yoke. Goya adapted Brueghel's use of the Flemish people to his own Spain as part of his expression of the liberal, democratic ideal.

Both Brueghel and Bosch were well represented in the royal collections. Bosch's ribald fantasies of demons and monsters had fascinated the gloomy fanatic, Philip II. That king imported them from his dominions in the Low Countries because he believed they served a moral purpose by reflecting the vices and follies of the times. As such, he thought they would be of use to the Counter-Reformation. Goya was drawing much inspiration from them at this period of his career. Their grotesque satire, to which the humorless Philip II was apparently oblivious, is reflected in Goya's *Caprichos*.

At the end of the year Jovellanos and Saavedra were forced out of office by Godoy. Both fell ill simultaneously of a strange disorder. The rumor was that they had been poisoned at Maria Luisa and Godoy's orders.

Goya felt it was time for him again to announce the forthcoming edition of his etchings.

8

The World of Fantasy and Imagination

Because there was no print shop in Madrid, Goya's *Capri-chos*, or "Fantasies," went on sale on February 6, 1799, at a perfume and liqueur shop on the first floor of the house at No. 1, Calle del Desengaño, where Goya was then living. There is an irony in the name of the street. It means "disillusioned," and disillusionment is the principal theme of the eighty etchings that comprise this spiritual biography of a man who had seen too much behind the scenes.

In an unpublished prospectus for the set Goya wrote that he had "chosen subjects that offer opportunities to ridicule and condemn the prejudices, impostures, and hypocrisies that time has dignified." All these, in their myriad aspects, he saw and symbolized as monsters, hobgoblins, the fearful creatures that swim under the waters of sleep.

In the course of his long planning of the set, Goya moved to number 43, the plate he had originally intended as the title page. It thus introduces the second section of the set, which is devoted to the supernatural. For a frontispiece to the entire collection Goya substituted a self-portrait.

Why he made this change is not certain. Probably he thought, or was advised, that for purposes of sale he would do better to amuse the purchaser first and instruct him later. The *Caprichos* was intended as a business venture.

But his original intention is clear from the prospectus. "The author," he wrote, "has not attempted to imitate the work of other people, or even to copy nature. The imitation of nature is as difficult as it is admirable—when successfully accomplished. Let us, therefore, admire a method that disregards nature and reveals to our eyes forms and movements that exist only in imagination. . . . Like the poet, the painter selects from the universe what he sees is best for his own purposes. In one figure created out of fantasy he can express circumstances and characteristics that nature scatters amongst a crowd of individuals."

Plate 43 is the pictorial expression of this philosophical and psychological analysis of the artist's mind and work. In a preparatory drawing of 1797, the etching is dedicated to *"ydioma universal,"* the universal language Goya considered pictorial art to be. Its title is "The Sleep of Reason Produces Monsters." Its subject is a man of the arts—possibly Goya himself—who has fallen asleep at his worktable, which is littered with pens and paper. Behind and above him swarm the birds of night—screeching owls with leering faces, followed by a cloud of enormous vampire bats. One witchlike owl grasps a pen in its talons, urging the sleeper to take it up and record what these evil visions have to tell him. A sinister cat, seeing through the darkness, lurks in a corner.

What is Goya communicating through this powerful symbol? In a philosophical sense, he says that when man evades reality—that is, fails to use his gift of reason—and trusts in false causes, he becomes the victim of falsity. Superstitions and prejudices flock down upon him like these baleful birds, torturing him with doubt and distrust, and depriving him finally of the reason he has not exercised. These creatures hate the light and shun it. To banish them, all man has to do is flash the torch of Reason at them.

Time is the great night that gives these birds of darkness shelter. A false premise grows falser as it grows older. It begets a hideous brood in the same way that superstition, the spawn of a false premise, begets prejudice. Prejudice, in turn, begets hatred, violence, destruction. Time must be checked by Reason, for Reason sees that nothing has meaning except in reference to a particular time and place. The individual must awaken to live in the individual moment of his immediate context in time and space, not in general Time, which has meaning only in the context of the past.

On the literal level, Goya is symbolizing Spain, which he saw haunted by the superstitions and prejudices of the

"The Sleep of Reason Produces Monsters," Plate 43 of Goya's *Los Caprichos*.

past. Spain, he says, is static with fear of the evil birds, not pressing forward. Society rots in its own stagnation. The king is asleep to his queen's venality; the nobility are asleep to the disintegration of their roots; the Church is asleep to the ineffectuality of its practices; the people are asleep to the oppression of their blind belief in all of them. "Tell the world," screeches the owl with the pen to the sleeping artist, "that we, only we nightmares, are real." But when the light of Reason has roused the artist, they will have vanished. He then can tell the world that they are illusions.

Psychologically, Goya is symbolizing the hideous transformations which past events undergo in the unconscious mind and the way in which they come tumbling out of the files of the mind when sleep relaxes the conscious censor that keeps them in order. These are the dreams which terrify until their jumble is reordered by the analysis of reason. Like the cat in Plate 43 and like the cat in Goya's portrait of little Don Manuel Osorio (page 101), the fantasies of the unconscious wait to pounce upon and tease the mind when it is off guard. The cat will destroy the beauty and the pleasure of the moment. Memories of past experiences peer through the sleep-darkened windows of the mind or lurk in its dark corners, waiting for a chance to pounce. To fear the past, Goya is saying, is to play a Halloween prank on oneself.

Throughout the *Caprichos* Goya is externalizing and thus putting into order the feelings he had too long kept buried. His perceptions had gone beneath the surfaces he had painted. Practical considerations had forced him to repress them. The fact that he began the *Caprichos* shortly after his grave illness shows how this repression may have brought that collapse upon him. He would, he knew, never completely recover his physical health, but he could regain a spiritual health, a psychological integrity. What he felt deeply he expressed in forceful symbols—the uni-versal language. Feelings that lay "too deep for tears" be-came believable fantasies; Goya's witches, goblins, super-natural monsters are truer than reality. Everything in the *Caprichos* is distorted from nature to express the truth Goya had found behind the veil of sense impression. He had become a mystic without knowing it.

In the unpublished prospectus Goya had declared that the *Caprichos* contained "no personal satire because that would spoil the object of art and the means art had placed in the hands of the artist." Yet the entire set is subjective, as any transformation of the artist's individual emotional experience into a universal one must be. Goya had been hurt by his God in the affliction of deafness. His revenge was to see the world of men as a caricature of what man could be, just as Goya himself was now a caricature of what he had been. He had rejected the euphemisms of charm for the brutality of truth. Instead of disguising the crude, rough *majos* as colorful pastoral-comedy figurines, he was now ripping off the disguises of the elegant aristo-crats in order to show their cruelty and hypocrisy. And to make clear that his engravings were caricatures, Goya de-veloped a new style of drawing for them.

The exaggerations of caricature are not far from the dis-tortions of nightmares. What we call a "sweet dream" is the fulfillment of a happy wish. The monsters of a "bad dream" are projections into semi-reality of wishes to hate and to destroy. What Goya had found false in the world he destroyed symbolically by caricaturing it. Through the power of his drawing he destroys for the spectator the same hatreds because, once objectified, like a caricature they appear funny.

Satire holds a mirror up to nature. The objective reflec-tion is not what the person gazing subjectively into the looking glass wishes to see. The wicked queen did not enjoy her mirror on the wall telling her that another was fairer than she. The *Caprichos* are mirrors of society much like Jonathan Swift's "reflections" in his *Gulliver's Travels*. There is, in fact, a parallel between this satire and Goya's *Caprichos*. Swift transformed degraded human beings into the repulsive Yahoos, and elevated horses, the Houyhn-hnms, above them. Goya pictures men as apes and donkeys (Plates 37–41).

In Goya's prints the Spaniards of 1799 saw what they did not wish to see. The *Caprichos* were not popular. In four years, only twenty-seven sets were sold, though the price was low—the equivalent of about twenty dollars apiece.

The first section of the series is devoted to satirizing and caricaturing the follies of society: the indifference with which women marry; the mistake of allowing children to believe in a bogeyman; indulging children until they grow up fools. Women cannot be virtuous when men are wicked, says another plate. Everyone wears a mask, pretending to be what he is not, yet only deceives himself. Women are deceptive, and men are too stupid to see through them. Duels are absurd. People torture themselves by believing in superstitious lore. Anything for money or pride or vanity, especially where women are concerned. Women treat men as they do poultry, plucking them, spitting them, chasing them out; and men devour women like hungry dogs. Extreme punishment and public shame, like that of the Inquisition, accomplish nothing, any more than does a sluttish mother's spanking her careless child. Teachers are no better than their pupils; the ranks of the so-called learned are filled with charlatans. Man is a slave to his possessions.

None of these observations is particularly original, nor

"Off they go, plucked,"
Plate 20 of Goya's *Los Caprichos*.

"What if he has broken
the jug?" Plate 25 of
Goya's *Los Caprichos*.

does any belong exclusively to the end of the eighteenth century. The violence with which Goya has expressed them, however, makes them as biting as the acid that dug their lines into the metal plates on which he drew them. Every stroke speaks of gullibility and stupidity and greed, or of grim pathos when Goya is depicting the victims of ignorance and intolerance. Nothing is said—for Goya's pithy captions are riddles—yet everything is said. Evil and injustice, guile and self-degradation are explicit in every symbolic scene, however innocuous it first appears.

It was not enough for Goya to depict his victims as travesties of humankind in their actions, he must show their minds as possessed by witches and demons and goblins. The second section, in which Goya took his symbols from the supernatural world, deals with the metaphysical side of life, as the first section dealt with the physical. Many of them defy verbal explanation as do the experiences of shock and horror. Goya is revealing the self-loathing of persons who discover that the conduct they believe admirable is motivated by antisocial self-interest.

These are the monsters produced by the sleep of Reason. As his caption to the final etching, Goya wrote: "When dawn breaks, the witches, the hobgoblins, the dreams, the phantoms fly away, each to his place. It is lucky that such creatures show themselves only in the dark of night. No one has yet discovered where they hide in the daytime. If one were to succeed in trapping some goblins and showing them in a cage on the Puerta del Sol, he would make a fortune."

Half our life, Goya is saying, is spent in darkness, where these obscure creatures dwell. Half our thoughts are possessed by them. We cannot exhibit the thoughts in the Puerta del Sol, yet our actions make them as visible as they are in these etchings of the dark wilderness of the senses.

"Wait until you have been anointed!" Plate 67 of Goya's *Los Caprichos*.

The plates are an exorcism of the demons of the unconscious. For once they can be seen and recognized for what they are, their power is gone. "No one has seen us," say the goblins of Plate 79. But they are visible if only one cares to look instead of try to conceal. The beings of Goya's otherworld are involved in the daily actions of this one. They cut their nails, have a drink after work, watch the time, take the oath of a profession, go riding, fight each other. They are very much and very ironically alive.

Goya was using the folklore of his time to express a universal unconscious. A hundred-odd years later, the supernatural he expresses pictorially in the *Caprichos* would be similarly defined in the less universal language of psychology. In Goya's day only tentative gropings had been made toward this explanation of man's inherited fears and guilt.

Joseph Addison had written in his *Pleasures of Imagination* that "when the brain is hurt by an accident, or the mind disordered by dreams or sickness, the fancy is overrun with wild, dismal ideas and terrified with a thousand hideous monsters of its own framing." José Luis de Munárriz, whom Goya painted, had translated Addison's essay into Spanish.

Johann Kasper Lavater, a Swiss mystic of the late eighteenth century, developed a system of physiognomy which purported to reveal character through a study of facial characteristics. He hoped to rid the world of vice by making it immediately apparent.

The Dreams (*Los Sueños*) of Francisco de Quevedo was so widely read that a new edition was required in 1791. Quevedo regarded dreams as the work of Satan, and dwelt on the infernal nature of man's inner world. He thought religion the only means by which man could be helped to see the evil of his ways.

Goya knew these theories. His deafness had increased his reading. When he disposed of his house in 1823, he had over two hundred volumes in his library. Goya was in line with the advanced thinking of his day. But he did not derive the dream world of the *Caprichos* from theories he got at secondhand. The etchings themselves are contributions to the theories we follow today.

The dream world which Goya created out of his own feelings he made a stage where the evils of society could be displayed in all their sickening pageantry. Once they were shown for what they were, Reason, Goya trusted, would abolish them. Man had only to awake in order to banish what distorted him and his society. The *Caprichos* were Goya's systematic contribution to the improvement of his world.

He was not discouraged by their lack of success in Spain. He was too mature to believe that society could be changed by a single appeal to Reason. But he was gratified to learn that they made him known abroad. By dint of their form they could be circulated as his paintings could not be. They spread his influence. Delacroix copied them, and Daumier was greatly influenced by them.

In 1803, at the suggestion of Godoy, Goya offered the plates of the *Caprichos* to King Charles IV, who accepted them. Possibly Goya's generosity was motivated by alarm at a warning that the Inquisition was about to examine the religious propriety of the etchings. One story is that Charles IV, through Godoy's influence, informed the Inquisition that he had ordered the *Caprichos,* thus squelching its interference. The king was less a puritan than his father.

Charles IV gave Goya's son Javier a pension of about $750 a year in return for the plates. It was a good bargain for Goya. Javier was an art student; the pension would allow him to study abroad. It ended when it was no longer needed—Javier never accomplished much—but was restored in 1816.

It has been claimed that some of the etchings of the *Caprichos* are specific satires on Charles IV (Plate 4, for example—the spoiled brat), or on Maria Luisa and Godoy (Plate 36—a prostitute and her client in a storm). It is doubtful that Goya would have particularized his irony; the suggestion came from Court gossipers. Certainly none of the unholy trinity—king, queen, Godoy—would have condoned the offer of the plates, or accepted it, if they had believed they were Goya's victims.

Others have recognized the Duchess of Alba in some of Goya's fickle women, especially Plate 61 (*Volaverunt:* "They have taken flight") and in the face of the harpy in Plate 19. In the first, Goya is satirizing the empty-headedness of women; in the second, the risks they take. If Goya felt any personal resentment against the duchess, he would hardly have taken such a cheap revenge. The faces in question are simply those of beautiful but vapid women, any number of whom Goya had known in the Court or met at fashionable *tertulias*.

It is thought also that the features of the two-faced woman in another etching, *The Dream of Lies and Inconstancy*, are those of the flirtatious duchess. Butterfly wings, a symbol of passion as well as of immortality, sprout from her heads as they do from the one of the witch-borne woman in *Volaverunt*. But, as the title plainly states, this is another dream picture, another version of "The Sleep of Reason."

The Dream of Lies and
Inconstancy.

The etching was intended for inclusion in the *Capri-chos*. Goya, however, destroyed the plate after pulling only one proof. Probably he regarded it as too private a reflection for publication, for the man whose face registers longing and despair is clearly Goya himself. Or he may have thought it overstated.

Goya is merely saying with ugly emphasis that faith in human values is misplaced. The crone (or old man?) on the right, with her indecent gesture, appears in one form or another throughout the *Caprichos*. She symbolizes the way in which old women pass on the tricks of their sex or trade to their daughters. She is another expression of Goya's idea that Time justifies evils by making them conventions.

In the foreground a snake is about to devour a toad while a mask grins evilly at the war between these primitive forms of nature. Man is no better than woman, and vice versa, Goya is repeating. The war between innocence and evil has gone on since the beginning of time.

In the background appears, probably for the first time in Goya's iconography, a monumental tower, a kind of ziggurat. It broods over the drama of the human beings at its base like Time itself. It symbolizes permanence in a world of change, truth in a world of errors, real values in the midst of false ones.

The concept of Time was playing a large part in Goya's thinking at this period. In one of his "mirror" drawings, a young girl recoils from her "reflection" in a looking glass that shows her a serpent writhing around a scythe, the symbol of destructive Time. It is a travesty of the reconciliation symbol of the caduceus (two serpents entwined about a winged staff), the symbol of healing medicine.

One of Goya's allegorical paintings represents *Spain, Time, and History*. A preparatory sketch for it includes a swarm of bats, as in "The Sleep of Reason," as if to underline the evil delusion of Time the destroyer. Time with a broom hovers behind the two crones of *¿Qué Tal?* ("Can this be I?"), in the Museum of Lille, Goya's ironic contrast to its charming companion piece of two young *majas* (*The Young Girls*) in the same museum. Later, Goya would paint on the wall of his dining room a horribly powerful expression of Saturn, the grim god of Time, devouring his children. Death, Time, Destruction—these are the monsters of the dark world of man's unconscious. Only man's reason can overcome them and rescue man from the oblivion, the disintegration of the ego, that he has dreaded since the beginning of existence. Once awakened, man's immortal spirit can soar beyond the grasp of the nocturnal creatures of despair. The power is in man, not in some external force. The last illusion to be overcome is the in-

Spain, Time, and History. *National Museum, Stockholm.*

vincibility of a time-bound universe. These conclusions are the treasure Goya has brought to the surface from his dive into the depths of human nature.

From the technical point of view, the *Caprichos,* as well as all of Goya's subsequent work in the field of graphics, are masterpieces of the engraver's art. Goya's technique was unorthodox and unsystematic. The old method of etching consisted of drawing the design with a needle on a metal plate covered with an acid-resistant ground. The acid in which the plate was submerged then bit into the metal where it had been exposed by the needle, and produced a clean, even line. Because the artist's hand moves rapidly as he draws on the ground (usually thin wax or varnish), the result is spontaneous, rather like a guiding sketch.

"¿Que Tal?" *Museum of Fine Arts, Lille.*

This method did not satisfy Goya. To give his etchings an additional dimension, he used the relatively new method of aquatint. This had been discovered in the seventeenth century by Hercules Seghers, a Dutch painter and engraver. Rembrandt had used it. It had later been perfected by the French engraver Jean Baptiste Le Prince.

In this process free particles of acid-resistant resin are distributed over the plate. The acid bites channels around these. The channels hold the ink and print from them in contrast to the irregular white islands of the unbitten plate. By biting and re-biting, the tone can be darkened. The artist can control the grain by increasing or lessening the distance between the plate and the sprayer from which the resin, in a solution of alcohol, is applied, or the mesh bag from which it is shaken. The effect is to give the etching

The Young Girls. *Museum of Fine Arts, Lille.*

a variation of tones, rather like a watercolor wash. These heighten the interest of the passages the artist wishes to emphasize. Plate 32 of the *Caprichos* is a good example; it is pure aquatint.

Goya never drew directly on a plate. (Toward the very end of his life, however, he did draw directly on the stone for a lithograph.) His design was transferred to the plate by dampening the paper on which it had been drawn and pressing it on the plate—naturally in reverse. All engravers have to work in reverse. The transfer Goya then traced over with an etching needle. Afterward he sometimes added a wash (*lavis*) which was applied like aquatint but without a grain.

After the plate was removed from the acid, Goya pulled a proof. He might retouch this as a guide to alterations he wished to make on the plate. For these changes he used a pointed steel instrument (drypoint) or a triangular one (burin). The drypoint would make a line like one drawn in ink on blotting paper—the "burr." It shaded the line. The burin gave a severe, deliberate tone to a line and tapered it to a point.

Then Goya would apply the aquatint. Sometimes he rubbed down the bitten grain with a burnisher to get half-tones and highlights, or to break down the etched lines for a soft, rich, blurred effect. The total result was an unparalleled richness of tone such as is produced by delicate watercolor washes or, on the other hand, by the impasto of opaque paint. It completely removes the stigma of mechanical reproduction from Goya's prints, making each one seem as if it had been done by the artist's very hand.

Goya had begun pulling proofs of the early plates of the *Caprichos* in 1796, working alone in an attic he hired for the purpose in the Calle de San Bernardino. Later he entrusted the printing of the second edition of 1806–7 to

Rafael Estève, a close friend of his, and the Court Engraver. Because Goya's own handwriting was poor, he engaged a scribe, Pedro Gómez, to engrave the captions. The ink of the earliest impressions has a reddish hue; that of the later ones is dark brown.

When the Church of San Antonio de la Florida was reopened on July 1, 1799, no one could doubt after seeing Goya's frescoes that he was the greatest painter in Spain. Manuel Godoy pressed Goya's claims to be made First Court Painter. The office had been vacant since the death of Francisco Bayeu because Charles IV wanted to save money. On October 31, the king gave in, and named Goya.

The appointment read: "His Majesty, wishing to reward your distinguished merit and to give in person a testimony that may serve as a stimulus to all in the profession of art, of how much he appreciates your talent and knowledge of the noble art of painting . . ." Goya's salary was to be the equivalent of about $3,500 a year, plus a travel allowance, and he was to be given the house of Mariano Maëlla, who had shared the post with Bayeu, after Maëlla died. Charles IV allotted Goya a seat in the royal coach, one of the highest honors he could bestow; and Maria Luisa made Goya a present of a little Velázquez. Goya wrote to Zapater: "The sovereigns are crazy about your friend."

Goya had sobered down. There would be no more palace pranks like the caricatures on the white stockings. He had his coat of arms—compiled with scant regard for the sanctity of heraldry—painted on the door of his carriage. He was definitely Don Francisco de Goya y Lucientes. He was talking primarily now to kings and princes.

They talked, in turn, to him. Charles IV, Goya wrote Zapater, had inquired most solicitously about the health of "little Paco" (Javier), who had had smallpox. In the autumn of 1799, the king invited Goya to the little residence of La Granja. Philip V had built and landscaped this retreat in imitation of Louis XIV's Versailles in order to remind him of the gay French Court life he had had to leave behind. By September 24, Goya had painted Maria Luisa in Spanish costume—she, too, was at last adopting majaism—and again on October 4, on her favorite horse, Martial. The queen loved the results. Even though Goya showed her wrinkled and withered and decaying in the "mantilla" portrait, he made her royally spirited in the equestrian one. So Charles IV had to be painted on horseback also. He loved the portrait so much that he told Goya to do "the portrait of all of us together."

When Godoy, following suit, invited Goya to the summer palace of Aranjuez in the chilly spring of 1800, he insisted that Goya keep his own coat on at dinner in the freezing rooms. Godoy even learned sign language so that he could converse with his deaf protégé at dinner and on carriage rides.

Goya painted Godoy on horseback too, but the portrait has been lost. All that survives of this April visit to Aranjuez is Goya's touching portrait of Godoy's pathetic wife, pregnant with a child she had no wish to bear her porcine mate.

Goya kept flitting between Madrid and Aranjuez—four journeys in all—to study Velázquez' *Las Meninas* in preparation for his own group portrait of royalty. By June 9, 1800, he had finished the preliminary sketches of the members of Charles IV's family. He set to work on the group portrait immediately thereafter.

The finished painting, which hangs in the Prado, is one of the world's masterpieces of art. The thirteen members of the royal family are gathered in the grand salon of Aranjuez. In the center, appropriately enough, stands the smarmy Queen Maria Luisa, holding in either hand her two youngest children, whose father was probably Manuel Godoy. Maria Isabella looks like her mother; little Don Francisco de Paula, in a vermilion suit like Don Manuel Osorio's, closely resembles Godoy.

The group at the left is dominated by the heir to the throne, the future King Ferdinand VII—stupid, vapid, sly, almost deformed in body. To his left is his younger brother, Don Carlos, who looks old for his years. On both, the Bourbon features are unmistakable. Behind the infante,

The Family of Charles IV. *Prado Museum, Madrid.*

PHOTO MAS, BARCELONA

his aunt, Maria Josefa, leers like a hag from the *Caprichos*. Goya has spared her nothing, not even the birthmark by her left eye. On the infante's right is his future bride, Maria Antonina of Naples; Goya painted merely a woman in Court dress to represent her, for he had not yet seen her.

Before the group on the right stands the pompous, foolish paterfamilias of this regal, yet obviously bourgeois, family. Over Charles IV's right shoulder peers the flabby face of his brother Don Antonio, like the halfwit drunkard such a family would try to conceal. The Infanta Carlota Joaquina is just a dainty profile beside him.

Only the two figures to the far right—Prince Luis of Parma and his wife, the Infanta Maria Luisa, holding her baby—look human, decent and, if not intelligent, at least sincere. In reality the Infanta Maria Luisa was physically deformed owing to a curvature of the spine. Perhaps out of regard for her youth and her recent motherhood, Goya hid this abnormality and painted her as tenderly as he did the pathetic Countess of Chinchón, Godoy's hapless wife.

Far in the rear at the left stands Goya himself at his easel. He may be there because Velázquez included himself in *Las Meninas,* or because he would increase the unlucky thirteen personages to fourteen.

All but Goya are in gorgeous Court dress, bedecked with jewels or decorations, an irony that makes their faces and figures all the more degenerate. The arrangement of the figures is completely natural, as if the family had assembled just before going in to Christmas dinner, and were unaware that any stranger was looking at them.

The monotony of the long horizontal line of figures is broken by the circular shadows cast by the light which comes from the left to focus on the queen. The sharp, almost glaring colors of the costumes contrasts with the soft outlines and the subdued background. Strangely, the color

and the atmosphere of space and light idealize these un-
idealistic people. Goya has told the truth about them, but
he has told it without hurting their feelings. Even they
could see themselves as they were, yet somehow better
than they knew they were.

At some date about this time Goya painted two other pictures by which all the world knows him, if for nothing else
—*The Naked Maja* and *The Clothed Maja*. For many
years the legend persisted that this fascinating woman reclining on a green sofa, her hands behind her black hair
and smiling invitingly at the spectator, was the Duchess of
Alba. Then on November 17, 1945, scholars exhumed
the body of Maria Teresa Cayetana. They found its measurements so utterly different that the intriguing story was
disproved.

In 1868, Mariano Goya, the painter's grandson, then
sixty-one years old (he died in 1874), who lived almost in
poverty in the village of Bustarviejo, recalled that a certain
Father Bavi had supplied Goya with the model. This priest
was known in Madrid as "El Agonizante" because of his
work among the lower classes. He would tend them in
their last illnesses and help them to die in the arms of the
Church. The priest discovered the young girl on his rounds
of mercy and brought her to Goya, who quickly recognized
that El Agonizante's work was not all hardship. The *Maja*
was definitely a *maja*.

Of the six greatest nudes in painting—Giorgione's *Toilet
of Venus*, Titian's two Venuses, Velázquez' *Venus with a
Looking Glass*, and Goya's *Naked Maja*—the first three are
goddesses first. Velázquez' is a lady. Goya's is Woman. Her
slim yet lusciously rounded contours; her pearly flesh; her
bewitching rosy face with dark, wide-spaced eyes gazing
into the spectator's soul; her almost pensive half smile make
it difficult to believe that she is in reality not real. The

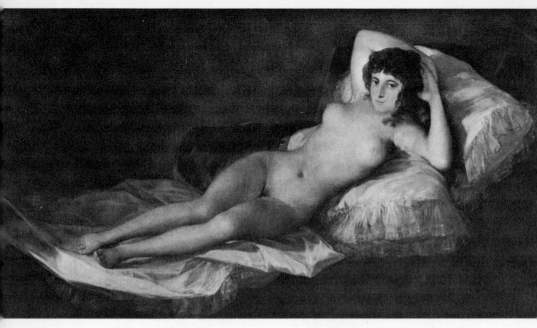

The Naked Maja. *Prado Museum, Madrid.*

The Clothed Maja. *Prado Museum, Madrid.*

effect is not a sense that art has outdone nature, but the wish that nature might imitate art. The wish is granted. No one after seeing *The Naked Maja* could envision an ideal woman in other terms than Goya's.

Ironically, *The Clothed Maja* is more sensuous, almost suggestive to the prurient. A nearly identical replica—except for the golden bodice, the pink sash, the white pajamas, and the golden slippers—it is a different conception of Woman. Perhaps the trick is the light. In *The Clothed Maja* it is reflected from the sheen of the pajamas. In *The Naked Maja* it is, as it were, absorbed into the glowing flesh. The one is thus separated from nature, whereas the other is part of nature.

The paintings were to get Goya into trouble. On March 16, 1815, a meeting of the Secret Chamber of the Inquisition decided that Goya should be summoned before their tribunal, identify the "immoral and abominable" *Majas* as his work, and explain why he had painted them, who had commissioned them, and for what purpose they were intended. It was a little late in the day for such an investigation, but the Inquisition had been reestablished by the reactionary King Ferdinand VII and was zealously making up for lost time. There is no record surviving of what happened, or even if Goya did appear before that dread tribunal. Presumably the king got him off.

However much Goya may have satirized Woman's character in the *Caprichos*, he was fully capable of recognizing and appreciating Her charms.

9

The Disasters of War

Once again a new order of things across the Pyrenees was threatening Spain. Napoleon Bonaparte had started to remake the map of Europe and was installing his tools as rulers of the areas he added to his empire. He offered the crown of the kingdom he was making out of Tuscany to Charles IV's and Maria Luisa's daughter, the Infanta Maria Luisa. She was to be queen of Etruria.

The royal parents loved that plan. The cultured, broadminded Mariano Luis de Uruquijo, who had temporarily replaced Manuel Godoy as Prime Minister, however, suspected Napoleon's motives, and opposed the move. Napoleon sent his brother Lucien to Madrid. Lucien gave Godoy a suit of damascened armor. Presently Uruquijo, whom Goya had painted quite literally as an "egg head," was kidnaped and tossed into prison.

Godoy returned to power in 1801 and, to please Napoleon, immediately declared war on Portugal—the ridiculous "War of the Oranges." Portugal soon capitulated and agreed to close its ports to England, Napoleon's chief adversary. As a reward, Godoy was made generalissimo of the Spanish forces on land and sea. He had to be painted in this new role, and as a victor.

Goya posed the royal favorite's bulk reclining on a sofa, then transformed in paint this soft couch into a hard rock, from which the generalissimo calmly and smugly surveys a scene of battle—flags, horses, and smoke—while perusing a military dispatch. An aide, presumably the Count of Teba, peers over Godoy's left shoulder. The portrait was finished by October 4, 1801.

A study for it is in the McCormick Collection in Chicago. (The completed work is in the Academy of San Fernando, Madrid.) All of Godoy's calculating opportunism is in Goya's interpretation of this dictator, of whom Napoleon on St. Helena would say: "That man was a genius." The vanquished emperor had good reason for the judgment. Godoy opened Spain to Napoleon's depredations.

Goya made a separate portrait of the Count of Teba in 1803 or 1804. Now in the Frick Collection, New York

Manuel Godoy. *Academy of San Fernando, Madrid.*

City, it is a keen psychological study of the brilliant, temperamental, rebellious young man. The count, who was an uncle of the future Empress Eugènie of France, published two treatises highly critical of Godoy and Charles IV, took part in the riot at Aranjuez that resulted in their downfall, and fought, but not too bravely, in the War of Independence (sometimes called the Peninsular War).

For the next few years Goya restricted his work to portraits of less distinguished persons, his friends, and his family. He could now afford to paint only whom he wished to. He had no interest in sitters from whose faces he could not abstract a statement about general human nature, no matter what he said about them as individuals. Everything in the canvas Goya designed to contribute to the drama of a human being impressing his personality on the world. Regardless of how the subjects are posed, they are full of this psychological action. They are vigorous characters in a novel that is a panorama, an encyclopedia of life itself— like *Tom Jones,* or *War and Peace,* or *Vanity Fair.*

Among them is the gorgeous Doña Isabel Cobos de Pórcel, in London's National Gallery, the epitome of the ideal Andalusian beauty, fiery and full of style.

Some are in American collections: Don Ignacio and Doña Josefa Garcini, in New York's Metropolitan Museum; Don Alberto Foraster, in the Hispanic Society of America, New York; Don Isidro González Velásquez, in a private collection in Boston; the (supposed) Countess of Gondomar, in the Detroit Institute of Arts; Don Tadeo Bravo de Rivera, in the Brooklyn Museum; Antonio Noriega de Bada y Bermúdez, in the National Gallery, Washington, D. C. Goya was also working out new ranges of color in this fruitful period. These works are among his finest.

Regardless of his increasing mastery of art, Goya was

outvoted in 1804, when the post of Director of the Academy of San Fernando fell vacant. It went to Gregorio Ferro, the same mediocrity who had won over Goya in the competition of 1766. Probably the voting members distrusted Goya's independence and his stormy disposition, and recognized the danger to themselves of entrusting an executive position to a genius.

The following year, in July, Javier married Gumersinda, the daughter of the rich, influential bourgeois of Zaragoza, Don Juan Martín de Goicoechea. It was a lucky match for

Doña Isabel Cobos de Porcel. *National Gallery, London.*

the son Goya adored but who had little of his father's ability or personality. Like many other sons of genius fathers, Javier was a nonentity, and a rather ungrateful, imperceptive one at that. In Goya's eyes, however, nothing was too good for his only child.

He made a handsome wedding portrait of Javier, depicting him as a dandy. Javier's sophisticated, self-confident pose is perhaps unconscious irony, for his face is clearly that of a tentative adolescent. All the father's pride in a son who has landed himself in a fine, upstanding family appears in this symphony of pearly gray, black, and white.

Goya apparently liked his daughter-in-law, for he painted a flattering portrait of her, giving her an almost oriental quality of beauty. In honor of the occasion Goya also painted Gumersinda's two sisters: Geronima, aged fifteen; and Cesarea, aged twelve. These three-inch-in-diameter miniatures are in the Rhode Island School of Design, Providence, Rhode Island.

The newlyweds came to live with Goya and Josefa in the new house Goya had bought. A month later, Javier and Gumersinda moved to lodgings of their own. Apparently life with Goya was a trial only Josefa could endure. Yet Goya had pledged himself to look after the new couple and their children, if any should come of the marriage. Only one child was born to them—Mariano, in 1807. It was one more disappointment to Goya to find that the son he loved and treated so generously could not be close to him.

In the early months of 1806 Spain was inflamed with alarm by its Public Enemy Number One—Pedro Pinero, called "El Maragato" from his hometown of Andinuela in the Margateria Mountains of the province of León in northwestern Spain. The newspapers of the time described the exploits of this highwayman with as much sensationalism as the American press of 1934 reported the movements of John Dillinger.

Javier Goya. *Collection of the Vicomtesse de Noailles, Paris.*

Maragato was captured and sentenced to death, but on April 26, 1806, he made a dramatic escape from the prison of Cartagena. For the next six weeks he terrorized the countryside, even though handicapped by a leg injury sustained when he had leapt over the forty-four-foot-high prison wall.

On June 10, Maragato appeared at a house in the Verdugal Mountains near Toledo. He demanded food and shelter, and, after he got it, locked up the occupants of the house in one room. While he was eating "very slowly and with much coolness and serenity of mind," as a contemporary pamphlet put it, there came to the door a mendicant Franciscan, Fray Pedro de Argaya, of Zaldivia. Maragato's charity was to lock up this monk with the other prisoners.

Before departing on the horse he planned to steal, Maragato remembered that he needed better shoes. He unlocked the door and demanded some.

Fray Pedro saw his chance. "Brother," he called to the bandit, "I have a good pair." He edged out of the room, grabbed the barrel of Maragato's gun, and after quite a struggle, wrested it from the brigand. Maragato started to run. Fray Pedro aimed low, and fired, wounding Maragato in the buttocks and legs so that he fell flat. The friar then tied him up.

Late that night the police finally arrived and took Maragato off to jail in the nearest town, Oropena. Troops were summoned, who eventually conducted him to the royal prison in Madrid. Later he was hanged on a public gallows.

Blind street singers and guitarists, like the Tío Paquete Goya painted, told the story to passersby who could not read the newspapers or could not afford the prints that reproduced the incidents. Songs and poems extolled the bravery of Fray Pedro and the crimes of Maragato. Even a minuet, titled "The Capture of Maragato," was advertised for sale.

Maragato Robs a Fat Purser

Maragato Points a Gun at Fray Pedro

Fray Pedro Captures Maragato's Gun

Fray Pedro Clubs Maragato

Fray Pedro Shoots Maragato

Fray Pedro Ties up Maragato

Goya jumped on this newsmongering bandwagon with six paintings on wood, arranged like an *aleluya*—a broadside with pictures in story sequence. These are now in the Art Institute of Chicago. Goya drew on the many popular prints of the time for his subject matter and for the faces of the friar and the robber, and he must have read the pamphlet. Apparently he made the paintings either for his own diversion between commissions, for he kept them, or for some *aleluya* that was never printed or has completely disappeared. They are examples of vivid narrative art, omitting nonessential details and concentrating on the most dramatic moments of the capture. As always with Goya, they are full of action, especially Number Four—the bandit and the friar wrestling for the gun. Goya obviously had fun painting them.

The excitement over the capture of Maragato soon dwindled to nothing. A larger threat to Spanish tranquility was looming in the diminutive shape of another robber, Napoleon Bonaparte. Napoleon was waiting only to secure the middle of Europe before attacking the Spanish peninsula. If he could add that to his dominions, he would control the coastline of Europe from Riga to Gibraltar to the Adriatic. The trade which supported his greatest enemy, England, would be ruined, and Britain could be crushed. After his victory over the Russians at Friedland (Pravdinsk) on June 14, 1807, Napoleon made Spain his next objective.

Godoy had lost any popularity he might have had with the Spanish people after the disaster at Trafalgar. The nobles were insulted by the way in which he had been elevated above them. After the Infante Ferdinand's plot to oust Godoy failed, Godoy's attempt to rouse Charles IV against his own son merely made the royalty-worshiping Spaniards hate Godoy more. When Napoleon's General Andoche Junot led French troops across the Pyrenees, the

Spaniards welcomed them as their deliverers from the hated Godoy. Actually Godoy had proposed resisting Napoleon, but the sovereigns thought that an insane idea. They preferred to try to escape to South America.

By March 17, 1808, the French army was near Madrid. A mob collected within the city, and the next day marched to Aranjuez, where the royal family were packing up to leave Spain. The mob surrounded Godoy's palace and broke into it. Godoy, half dead from thirst during his thirty-six hours' hideout rolled up in a rug in the attic, was dragged before his archenemy, the Infante Ferdinand.

To save his favorite prime minister, Charles IV put Godoy into protective custody in a prison cell. Then Charles abdicated in favor of Ferdinand, whom the mob demanded as king.

Napoleon, wanting no trouble from Spain, dispatched his brother-in-law, Joachim Murat, to follow up Junot's army, which was proceeding to subjugate Portugal. With great military pomp Murat entered Madrid on March 23 to keep order there with his own troops, twenty-five thousand strong.

The following day, Ferdinand, now King Ferdinand VII, quietly entered the city. He was greeted with joy by the loyal Spaniards, who called him *el rey idolatrado* ("the idolized king"). Ferdinand returned the compliment by giving a sizable sum of money to the poor, opening the royal parks to hunting, and lowering the price of tobacco.

At the request of the Academy of San Fernando, Ferdinand sat for a portrait by Goya. On April 5, and on another day, he posed for a total of forty-five minutes—too short a time for even Goya to realize the ambitious plans he had for an equestrian portrait of "Ferdinand the Desired." Before Goya could finish the painting, Ferdinand was in exile at Valençay, in France.

Napoleon had summoned Charles IV and Maria Luisa

to Bayonne, a seaport some thirty miles north of the Spanish border. They went in one-hundred-year-old carriages under a French escort, expecting that Napoleon would reinstate them on the throne of Spain. Napoleon also sent for Godoy, who he thought would aid him in his next move, and for Ferdinand.

Maria Luisa, Napoleon wrote his minister, Talleyrand, "wore her heart and her history on her face, which is beyond imagination." The old king he thought honest. Ferdinand he put down as stupid and sly. All the family behaved abominably to one another.

Napoleon informed them that it was not in his interest for any Bourbon whatever to occupy the throne of Spain. He offered the Bourbons before him a refuge in France and a small allowance. Godoy he exiled to Rome. Then Napoleon announced that his brother, Joseph Bonaparte, would be king of Spain.

The Spaniards did not know this yet—the agreement yielding all Bourbon rights to Napoleon was not to be signed until May 5—but they knew they had no love for any usurper like Joachim Murat. They began attacking his officers. By April 1, Murat was scared. He complained to Napoleon, who rebuked him for thinking so much about the "rabble of Madrid." By May 1, the aggrieved Murat wrote his imperial brother-in-law that there was no rioting any longer in Madrid.

The very next day there was. A report got around the city that the rest of the royal family—feeble-minded Don Antonio, the queen of Etruria, the Infante Don Francisco de Paula—were being hustled off. Charles IV had sent for them to join him at Bayonne. Prince Francisco de Paula, the vermilion-suited child of Goya's family portrait, was crying, a footman reported, because he did not want to leave his home and country. That was enough to inflame the populace. About nine in the morning the cry went up that their darling little *infantido* was being kidnaped by the French.

The mob attacked. The French guarding the carriages which had been assembled for the royal exodus fired on them. Murat, cowering in his study, ordered a battalion to clear the square before the palace.

The mob withdrew, only to reform, now some twenty thousand strong, in the Plaza Mayor. Any French soldier they found they shot or stabbed. The Madrileños who remained indoors fired on the French from windows. In the hospitals Spanish nurses finished off the wounded French who had been carried there.

The mob fell back before the French cavalry, and regrouped in the Puerta del Sol. From the windows of his house on that square Goya could have seen the slaughter.

Then came the Mamelukes, Napoleon's oriental cavalry. Swinging scimitars, they looked like Moors, the long-hated enemies of Christian Spaniards. The frenzy of the mob reached a new peak. Well-nigh helpless themselves, they nevertheless fell on the Arabs, stabbing the horses from below, then dragging the riders from the saddles and killing them. The Mamelukes were losing until they were reinforced by the Fusiliers of the Guard, commanded by Colonel Friedrichs.

The commander of the Spanish troops in Madrid disobeyed orders and put the few cannons in the barracks at the disposal of the mob's leaders. But this help was of little use against the superior numbers and arms of the French. By nightfall the insurrection had been put down. Only a few desperate fanatics went on fighting in the narrow streets of the Lavapié section.

Murat's reprisals, carried out by General Grouchy, were merciless. All night long and into dawn of the following day, May 3, the insurgents who had been rounded up were driven before French firing squads and shot. Anyone found with so much as a penknife was proscribed. The streets ran with blood; the open spaces were piled with dead.

It was six years before Goya dared to put on canvas his impressions of the charge of the Mamelukes, and of the executions of the rebels which he could easily imagine from the volleys of gunfire reverberating all through that dreadful night. By 1814, the French had been driven out of Spain, and Ferdinand VII was back on the throne. On February 24, 1814, Goya wrote to the government, expressing his "ardent desire to perpetuate by means of painting the most remarkable and heroic actions and scenes of our glorious insurrection against the tyrant of Europe." He also asked for financial assistance to do so, and received a grant on March 9. Goya's two paintings—*The Second of May, 1808* and *The Third of May, 1808*—hang side by side in a basement gallery of the Prado, ironically the same room that includes Goya's sentimental *Crucifixion*.

The charge of the Mamelukes (*The Second of May*) is, if nothing else, a remarkable demonstration of how art can make order from disorder. The composition—all vertical and horizontal lines—is dramatic because of this contrast alone. Three charging horses meet a line of three citizens on foot. Prone dead bodies stretch in opposite directions to the horses' movement. The daggers slash down and across. The thrust of the central horse's hindquarters is resisted by the thrust of the combatants' legs.

The action and counteraction of thousands Goya has abstracted into the five figures of the first plane and the six of the second plane. The others are suggested by blurred heads, while the long perspective of the wall indicates thousands more, massed almost to infinity. The red of blood and the red of costume contrast dramatically with the green of the "white" horses and of the citizens' jackets. The whole canvas is infused with fury. The citizen just to the left of center has stabbed once and will stab again. The eyes of the horses are glazed with terror. The French commander fiercely waves his battalion forward to fresh slaughter.

The scene of the executions (*The Third of May*) is a Calvary of tragedy. The principal figure, livid in the pitiless light of the square lantern, raises his arms as if he were nailed to a cross. He stares defiantly at the stark line of fusiliers, their faces hidden—the shameful injustice of revenge. Blood streams from a heap of previous victims. A monk prays; another victim pleads piteously; a third hides his face in his hands. Up the hill of sacrifice are being

The Second of May, 1808. *Prado Museum, Madrid.*

herded the next victims, deprived of all dignity. The line of them stretches back and back toward the walls of the city. Countless human lives are being offered to gratify the thirst for blood of an impersonal, tyrannical god. Over the scene broods a dark, dense sky.

The painting compels the spectator to listen and become involved. Goya is preaching the new gospel of reason and enlightenment, that every man has a right to his individuality and to justice. Goya puts the spectator face to face with the horrible in his world, however unwilling the viewer may be to see it.

In *The Third of May, 1808* not only does an actual contemporary event enter the field of art for perhaps the first time, but that event is placed in the context of human rea-

The Third of May, 1808. *Prado Museum, Madrid.*

PHOTO MAS, BARCELONA

son and morality. From then on, art could ask questions, not merely make statements. It ceased to be an ornament of life, a decorative comment, or even an interpretation. It became a challenge. It calls on man to assert himself against the tyranny of the superstition that he is at the mercy of a supernatural force. He shall not be punished without having had a voice in the decree of judgment. From the blood of the martyrs of May 3, 1808, must spring a new world of freedom and of each man's right to the pursuit of happiness. There must be no more rigid, impersonal firing squads.

The victims of the ruthless suppression of the May 2 insurrection did not die in vain. The bloody riots of Madrid inspired the Spanish people throughout their country to resist and destroy the hated invaders. The Spanish army was puny and useless. The Spanish people were too independent to be good soldiers, but they were magnificent guerrillas. The pride that made them hate obeying orders gave them the courage to fight alone or with a few who felt the same as they.

Napoleon failed to distinguish between the ill-equipped Spanish army, commanded by senile and ignorant aristocrats, and the Spanish people—an example of the unseeing tyranny against which Goya was inveighing. Soon Napoleon found it almost impossible to maintain any system of communications with his forces. Messages failed to arrive, for the Spaniards would capture their bearers and kill them, leaving the naked, mangled bodies about the countryside as a kind of warning. The guerrillas were a terror by night to the French. The invaders grew demoralized by the stealthy attacks on them as they slept; they would awake to find half their comrades with their throat slit.

While this guerrilla warfare was avenging the massacre of May 2-3, the puppet king, Joseph Bonaparte, arrived in

Madrid on July 31, 1808. The citizens greeted him with lugubrious silence. Nine days later, he left. The Madrileños went wild wth rejoicing. A surprise victory over the French at Baylen, in Andalusia, encouraged their hopes. A collection was taken up to provide the ragged army with better equipment. Goya contributed to it.

On August 25, 1808, Ferdinand, who had been swindled out of his throne by Napoleon, was proclaimed king of Spain in exile by the Spanish parliament. By then Goya had finished his equestrian portrait of his sovereign. Later he gave it gratis to the Academy, which nevertheless paid him a token sum for it.

Meanwhile, the French were besieging Zaragoza in earnest after their first detachment—Poles—had penetrated its walls, only to be driven out by the murderous populace. All through July, 1808, the French bombarded the city, which was defended by Don José Palafox, a twenty-eight-year-old officer of the Royal Guard.

It was then that the twenty-year-old Maria Augustina saw her lover fall beside the cannon he had been firing at the enemy. The French guns had driven all the other Spanish cannoneers from their positions on the walls of Zaragoza. Maria Augustina ran to the side of her dying fiancé, snatched the fuse from his hand, and fired the cannon. The sound recalled the retreating Spaniards. They rushed back to their posts and reopened fire until the French ceased the attack.

Goya was to depict her heroism in Plate 7 (*What Courage!*) of *The Disasters of War*.

All through July the heroic defense of Zaragoza lasted until the French bombardment had destroyed the walls. The French entered the city on August 4. At the bottom of French General Verdier's note demanding capitulation, Palafox scrawled, "War to the knife!" It was to become the

Spaniards' rallying cry and motto. The Zaragozans took it literally. Men, women, and even children fell upon the French as they forced their way through the streets, destroyed some five hundred of them, and wounded fifteen hundred more.

Palafox sent for Goya to come to Zaragoza to see the ruins of the city and paint them for propaganda purposes. It would be a perilous journey for the sixty-two-year-old painter, but, as he wrote in reply, it was something "from which I could not turn away because of the great interest I have in the glory of my fatherland."

As a companion on this trip through the war-torn countryside, Goya took along his pupil, Luis Gil Ranz. Once they were stopped by French soldiers and questioned. Goya's deafness made the French think him a spy. He was almost shot. Ranz rescued him and hid him for a time in his own village of Renales. They did not reach Zaragoza until October.

Goya's keen observation took in every aspect of the devastation of the city and the desolation of the country. He made many drawings of the scenes of war. These, which Palafox hung in his study, were destroyed when the French reattacked Zaragoza in January and February, 1809. Only one has been described, a scene of boys dragging dead French soldiers through the public square on August 4, 1808. But they did not vanish from Goya's mind. Abstracted and charged with powerful feelings, they reappeared in Goya's savage indictment of war, the series of etchings known as *The Disasters of War*.

It was a sad trip for Goya. The destruction appalled him and grieved him as if it were the end of his world. It was the ironic antithesis of the creativity that was his life, the only thing that makes life bearable because it alone is fruitful.

It was the last time he was to see Martín Zapater. Their correspondence had come to an end some seven years before, but their friendship was as strong as ever. Together they went to Fuendetodos. Goya saw again the first work he had ever shown the public. He could not believe he had painted it.

Trapped by the second siege of Zaragoza, Goya remained in Fuendetodos until after Zaragoza capitulated on February 20, 1809. Then he returned to Madrid, to find himself in an equivocal position. The city had surrendered to Napoleon in person on December 3, 1808. Joseph Bonaparte, *el rey intruso* ("the intruder king"), had returned in January, 1809. His tenure had been confirmed by the Treaty of Vienna, and he began to rule in earnest by decreeing that all holders of government offices must take an oath of allegiance to him. The order included Goya, as First Court Painter under the previous regime; but Goya was absent from Madrid at the time, and never took the oath.

Goya did, however, accept a commission to paint King Joseph (José I). Although now a man of some substance, Goya was in financial straits. The commission had been procured for him by his friend Don Tadeo Bravo del Rivero, the Peruvian lawyer and Commissioner of Madrid. (Rivero's portrait, by Goya, painted in 1806, now hangs in the Brooklyn Museum, New York.) The king's portrait was to be the City of Madrid's honor to the new sovereign. Goya was paid the equivalent of about $1,000 for it. But Goya was never officially connected with Joseph's Court.

Goya solved the ticklish problem of loyalty in his design for an allegorical work that still hangs in Madrid's Town Hall. He signed the agreement for it on December 23, 1809, and had it finished by February 27, 1810, so that it could be unveiled on St. Joseph's Day, March 19. A *maja*, representing "Madrid," leans on the shield of the city and points to a frame held by winged figures. Above this hover two other winged creatures, one blowing a trumpet and the other bestowing a wreath. Inside the frame Goya painted a likeness of King Joseph that he had copied from an Italian engraving. The painting, quite out of key with the style Goya had been following for several years by then, is far from his best work. Goya was no more at home in the field of allegory than he was in that of mystical religion.

The *Allegory of the City of Madrid* had a curious subsequent history. In 1812, the portrait of Joseph was scraped off by some hack after that monarch's fall, and the word *Constitución* painted in to commemorate the adoption of a democratic form of government in Spain. Then, after

Allegory of the City of Madrid. *Ayuntamiento, Madrid.*

PHOTO MAS, BARCELONA

Ferdinand VII had suppressed the constitution in 1823, his portrait, by Vicente Lopez, filled Goya's frame. Sixty years later, the Council of the City of Madrid was asked to have the tryannical Ferdinand's face removed, since it was a bitter memory. The present words *Dos de Mayo* ("Second of May") were painted over it to commemorate a more glorious episode in the city's history.

The constitution was largely the inspiration of Jovellanos. King Joseph had asked him to be Minister of the Interior. Jovellanos refused, and joined the Patriotic Party. He was chosen a member of the Central Junta, a makeshift national government that coordinated the efforts of the provincial juntas to continue guerrilla resistance to the French invaders.

The leaders of the Central Junta agreed to make an alliance with England for the purpose of driving out the French. Twelve thousand English troops, under the future Duke of Wellington, had disembarked in Portugal on August 1, 1808, to liberate that country, which Junot had subdued for Napoleon, and to continue into Spain. Half the members of the Junta, however, wanted an absolute monarchy under Ferdinand VII; the other half wanted a constitution.

They met at Cádiz to draft one. It was then that the term "liberal," as it is used today in reference to political opinions, was coined. The *liberales* saw liberty as an ideal worth dying for. Their opposites, the *serviles*, thought Napoleon a destroyer of religion, for on December 4, 1808, he had suppressed the Inquisition and secularized the convents and monasteries.

The liberals hoped that Napoleon, whose policies King Joseph naturally rubber-stamped, would put their ideals into practice. In the same decree of December 4, 1808, Napoleon had abolished feudal rights and courts of justice, and the provincial customs duties which the feudal lords had imposed on goods coming into their territories. The constitution drafted in Cádiz embodied all these liberating measures. It also provided for popular sovereignty without denying Ferdinand's rights to the throne; for individual freedom; for freedom of speech and of the press; for the separation of the executive and the judicial branches of the government. It was, in short, a manifesto of all the political thinking which had already enlightened the United States of America and France.

Goya sympathized with these ideals. They were not only those of his friends and intellectual mentors—Jovella-nos; the poets Leandro Fernándaz de Moratín and Juan Antonio Meléndez Valdés; and Bernardo de Iriarte—but also his own conviction that the end of history was for man to be free to live in truth as he saw and found it. Joseph I, furthermore, was doing things that pleased Goya. He restored the bullfights Godoy had forbidden; he loved and patronized the theater, which both Charles III and Charles IV had ignored; he was beautifying Madrid.

On the other hand, Goya could not forget that he him-self was a Spaniard and that French invaders were killing his countrymen and devastating his country. He had no wish to collaborate with the French. In 1811, Joseph awarded him the Royal Order of Spain, which he had established—called by loyal Spaniards "The Order of the Eggplant" to ridicule it—but Goya never wore its red cravat. Still, Goya painted pro-French Spaniards—the afrancesados—and French General Nicolas Guye. The por-trait is in the collection of Mrs. Marshall Field, New York City. It is a splendid work with a crisp touch and a rich, dark tone.

Goya could not resist doing, also in 1810, a portrait of the General's little nephew, Victor, a page to Joseph Bona-

Victor Guye. *National Gallery of Art, Washington, D.C., Gift of William Nelson Cromwell.*

parte. This charming painting is now in the National Gallery, Washington, D. C. It shows a blue-eyed boy with reddish gold hair, holding an open book to which he is paying no attention. Instead he is staring solemnly at the spectator unsentimentally and, therefore, all the more appealingly.

Another sympathizer with the French, and the one whom loyal Spaniards hated most, was General José Manuel Romero. Goya's portrait of this severe and sinister, but impressive, minister who held several portfolios under King Joseph, is in the collection of Mrs. Chauncey McCormick, in Chicago. The general's splendid uniform appears too big for him, as if Goya wished to show that he thought Romero a man of straw.

The conflict of interests caused Goya much spiritual agony. He vented it in wildly expressionistic drawings and paintings of assaults, rapes, and murders. Such is the grisly *Hanging of a Monk* in the Art Institute of Chicago, a fine piece of expressionism. These form a narrative of the efforts and the humiliations of the creative, the upright, and the innocent who are kept in bondage by tyranny and fanaticism. Pessimistic in tone, they show Goya's feeling that the triumph of Freedom and Truth is but a dream. Even so, his divided loyalties affected his health. They kept being tested.

On October 25, 1810, for example, he was appointed along with the painters Mariano Maëlla and Manuel Napoli, members of the Academy, to select fifty paintings representative of Spanish art for Napoleon to send to his museum. Twenty years earlier Goya had been directed to catalogue the paintings of the Royal Collection, and so knew them well. He fooled the emperor by choosing works by minor painters and, from those of the masters, poor canvases or copies.

They did not reach their destination until 1813. The disappointed Director of the Musée Napoléon declared that only six could be exhibited. "One can easily see by this choice," he wrote, "how much His Majesty the King of Spain has been deceived by those persons whom he had charged with the care of selecting them."

Much of the time Goya spent on another series of etchings. These were not published until 1863, when they were given their present title by the Academy—*The Disasters of War*. But one of the few sets printed by Goya during his lifetime he gave to his friend Ceán Bermúdez, with the title: "Fatal Consequences of the Bloody War against Bonaparte in Spain, and other Emphatic Caprices."

Goya worked on them on and off from 1810 until 1820,

often being out of materials, such as metal plates, because of war shortages. By the time he had finished them, there was no interest in realistic pictures of a war everyone was trying to forget. Hence, Goya did not publish them, for he did not want a popular failure like that of the *Caprichos*. He gave the plates to Javier, who stored them until he gave them to the Academy.

The Disasters may have had no appeal to the Spaniards of 1820, but to the people of today they speak eloquently of the horrors of all wars. Probably the most effective pieces of antiwar propaganda ever produced, they perhaps serve their purpose better in a world for which war has lost every vestige of adventure, romance, and glory. Certainly there is no trace of any of these former attitudes toward war in Goya's eighty-three exposures of war's hideous futility.

The series opens with a kneeling ragged man, his arms outstretched in cruciform appeal like the victim of the firing squad in *The Third of May, 1808*. Its title is "Sad Premonitions of Things to Come." The series ends with two plates of an idealized woman lying dead. "Truth Is Dead," says the first caption; "Will She Rise Again?" is the title of the last.

A few plates previous to the final one, number 69 shows a skeleton above which hovers a swarm of Goya's creatures of the night. A bony finger clutches a pen which has written on a tablet a single word, *Nada* ("Nothing").

The Bishop of Granada is said to have seen this etching at Goya's house, and to have exclaimed: "How sublime an idea! Vanity of vanities, all is vanity."

"How well you have understood me!" Goya replied. "My man has returned from the grave to tell us that he has made the great journey and has found nothing, even down there."

This sense of futility pervades the entire set, even those

plates that express courage and heroism. Goya is always asking "Why?" Why are dead men's limbs cut off (Plate 39)? Why does a French soldier stare smugly at a guerrilla hanged from a shell-shattered tree (Plate 36)? Is it with reason, or without, that two guerrillas, armed with knife and pike, attack two grenadiers (Plate 2)? Of a man vomiting on a heap of dead, Goya asks: "Is this what you were born for?" (Plate 12). Or just plain "Why?" or "What more can be done?" of the ghastly scenes of Plates 32 and 33.

Shootings and hangings, rape and murder, pillage and the abandonment of children, cynical mutilations of the dead, and burials—these are what war means. Human dig-

"Sad premonitions of things to come," Plate 1 of Goya's *The Disasters of War*.

nity has vanished, whether of the Spanish guerrilla or of the French invader. Goya does not take sides. To him all makers of war are monsters. Only the helpless victims are to be pitied, such as the women and children who starved in the famine that struck Madrid in the winter of 1811–12 (Plates 58–61).

The makers of war are the blind leading the blind (Plate 70—one of the "emphatic caprices"). A demonic angel records war's annals (Plate 71). The priests who preach war's honor are walking a tightrope or are charlatans (Plates 77 and 75). The government is an obscene carnivorous vulture (Plate 76). War is for animals alone (Plate 78).

"Great heroism—against dead men!" Plate 39 of Goya's *The Disasters of War.*

The uniforms and the costumes and the pieces of artillery pin *The Disasters* to a certain date no more than archaic phraseology dates the meaning of the Bible. Goya has eluded his enemy, Time. For the depths of degradation to which man, made only a little lower than the angels, can sink is timeless. The hair-raising fruit of Goya's trees and the gas ovens of Auschwitz were both created by man. In *The Disasters of War* Goya unleashes his fury at these obscenities.

"This I Saw" is the title Goya gave to Plate 44; and to the following one, "This I Also Saw." They are etchings of refugees. Many of the subjects for *The Disasters,* it can be assumed, Goya did see with his own eyes, probably on his trip to Zaragoza in 1808, during the subsequent months he remained in Fuendetodos, and during the famine in Madrid. Goya said that quickness to observe and retentiveness of vision were the essential qualities of a draughtsman. Only those who understood and remembered could be called artists. They should need no more time for observing the five cardinal points involved in a man's fall from a roof than was consumed by the fall itself.

Goya is said frequently to have stated that any artist who deserved the name should be able to reproduce from memory, with brush or pencil, the essential features of any scene or incident after having once seen it.

The year 1811 was a horrible one in Madrid. Over twenty thousand people died of starvation and disease between September of that year and August, 1812. Corpses lay in the streets. The very air stank of death. Goya had made his will on June 3, 1811. But it was Josefa, not he, who died, probably as a result of the famine, on June 20, 1812. Goya was left miserable and desolate in a country ravaged by the disasters of war.

10

The Anguish of a Reasonable Man

The war had brought three French armies to Spain. Arthur Wellesley, Lord Wellington, who had held Portugal for the British since 1809, knew that if these armies combined against him, he would be lost. In the early months of 1812, however, he began getting reports that Napoleon was siphoning off his veterans from the Peninsular Army for use in the campaign he was planning against Russia. Encouraged by these bulletins, Wellington decided to take the offensive, though he had under 55,000 men versus the 350,000 the French could throw against him.

Wellington captured the forts of Ciudad Rodrigo and Badajoz, which controlled the roads into Spain, and marched north to Salamanca, where he won a decisive victory over the French on July 22, 1812. The battle, which the Spaniards called Arapiles, marked the turning of the tide against Napoleon's far-flung armies.

Goya may have witnessed the engagement. The English and the French armies had been facing each other for two weeks before combat was actually joined. During this period Goya may have gone to Salamanca in the hope of being an eyewitness to a battle. It is said that on the very night of the engagement the victorious general was persuaded to sit to Goya for a portrait.

Wellington had no use for artists. After the battle he

was exhausted, cold—there had been an unusual change in the weather—and in pain from a bullet bruise on his thigh. It seems unlikely that he would have consented to pose. Yet a note, probably written by Javier Goya, on a red-crayon sketch of the general reads: "Drawing done in Alba de Tormes after the Battle of Arapiles of the Duke of Wellington from which the portrait was made." The drawing shows a man haggard and gaunt, ill-shaven and rumpled. The Iron Duke actually seems to be exhibiting some emotion.

It is more likely that Goya made the drawing after Wellington had arrived in Madrid on August 12. King Joseph had fled two days earlier. The capital welcomed the British general as a liberator. The tumultuous reception he got could have unsettled Wellington, who thought little of such displays of feeling and cared less whether the Spanish were "free" or not.

From the sketch, now in the British Museum, London, Goya made at least three finished portraits. The best is the one which was stolen from the National Gallery, London, on August 1, 1961, after the British government had bought it from an American collector for $392,000. It was recovered on May 22, 1965. An awkward equestrian portrait is in Apsley House, London. This was publicly exhibited at the Academy of San Fernando on September 2, 1812. A third, inscribed "A. W. Terror Gallorum" (Arthur Wellesley—or Wellington—the terror of the French) is in the National Gallery, Washington, D. C. In all of them Goya skillfully removed the tense lines of fatigue from the conqueror's face and depicted him as haughty and masterful.

Wellington did not wait to see his portrait displayed at the Academy, but retreated to the Portuguese frontier. King Joseph, who had now earned the nickname of Pepe

Botello (Joe Tosspot), returned to Madrid in December. Goya, who had no use for drunkenness, which was rare among Spaniards anyway, was in an even more ticklish position vis-à-vis his Majesty for having painted Wellington. He had also painted the guerrilla leader Juan Martín, called *El Empecinado* ("The Indomitable"), who had marched into Madrid at Wellington's side.

At the end of six months, during which Goya kept very quiet, the situation improved. Napoleon's disastrous campaign in Russia forced him to call more and more troops from Spain to France to defend its borders. Wellington reentered Spain and captured Burgos. Napoleon wrote his brother to remember he was a soldier and forget he was a king, to leave Madrid, and to concentrate his forces at Valladolid.

Joseph was only too glad to oblige. He had never wanted to be a king; Napoleon had forced him to be, and he was Napoleon's second choice at that. On March 17, 1813,

The Duke of Wellington. *National Gallery of Art, Washington, D.C., Gift of Mrs. P. H. B. Frelinghuysen.*

Joseph left Madrid forever, to command the French army. Along with him went carriage after carriage laden with loot, including art treasures and all the funds left in the treasury. He was headed for the Pass of Roncesvalles (Puerto Ibañeta) in the Pyrenees and for safety in France.

Wellington's army overtook him at Vitoria on June 20. Each of the armies was about seventy thousand strong, but the French were strategically at a disadvantage. Joseph, furthermore, had long since ceased giving orders, and no subordinate dared give them for him. It was a hopeless defeat for the French. Joseph left all his treasure behind and, with the survivors of the battle, ran for dear life toward the mountains and home.

At the end of March, 1814, Ferdinand returned to his homeland as King Ferdinand VII. Napoleon had offered to reinstate him, and the Spanish people were delighted to have him back. Ten days later, Napoleon himself abdicated.

The first thing Ferdinand did was to declare the constitution of 1812 null and void, and to dissolve the parliament. The next thing he did was to take violent measures against all Spaniards suspected of collaboration with the French.

Again Goya trembled. He was a well-known sympathizer with the liberals, many of whom had fled with the French to avoid just such reprisals as Ferdinand was now instituting. He had received King Joseph's Order of the Eggplant; it might be hard for him to prove that he had never worn it. Lest his property be confiscated, he prudently made it over to Javier, including the paintings he had kept at home. He reserved for himself only his cash.

Among the pictures was the portrait of the Duchess of Alba, now in the Hispanic Society of America, New York City; probably the portrait of the bullfighter José Romero, now in the Philadelphia Museum; and the lovely *Majas on a Balcony,* now in the Metropolitan Museum of Art, New York City.

There was also the strange, symbolic *Colossus*—a giant in the light of early evening, whose muscular bulk has caused people and animals to scatter in terror through the twilight. The figure was to appear again in Goya's work, in a magnificent mezzotint; in the *Proverbs;* and in a red-chalk drawing of Gulliver chained by the Lilliputians.

The giant is another of Goya's dream figures. It seems a projection of himself, whose genius towered above the petty ideas of lesser mortals, and whose glimpses of truth frightened the superstitious. It is his revenge on the insignificant who would harass and try to confine him.

Goya did everything he could think of to prove that he was, and had been, on the side which had now won. He applied for and received a grant to paint the scenes of resistance to the French on May 2 and 3, 1808. In only three hours he knocked off a portrait of the restored king to be used as a transparency in the illuminations that greeted Ferdinand VII on his triumphal entry into Madrid in May, 1814.

Goya also painted General José Palafox, who was posing as the hero of the resistance of Zaragoza, though the credit really belonged to the peasant leader, Tío Jorge Ibort. Palafox had ridden beside Ferdinand when the king entered Madrid. The equestrian portrait of Palafox is a fine piece of bravado military display, but a mediocre work of art. Goya never managed to understand horses or dogs well enough to paint them successfully. Yet, like his master Velázquez, he frequently introduced them into his compositions.

Goya was in financial straits again. Under King Joseph I, he had received no salary, having refused to be First Court Painter to that monarch. Palafox apparently had expected to receive the portrait as a gift. Goya had to insist on a price of one hundred doubloons (the equivalent of about $1,600). After Palafox refused to pay it, Goya kept the picture and transferred its ownership to Javier.

Nevertheless, Goya was indicted for collaboration by King Ferdinand's Tribunal of Rehabilitations on November 4, 1814. He was summoned to a hearing before Gonzalo de Vilchas, president of the commission. On the following April 14, the commission heard testimony on Goya's loyalty from Don Manuel Fernández Gamboa, of the Royal Council; Don Fernando de la Serra, Director-General of the Post Office; Don Antonio de Gamir, of the Council of the Indies; and Don Antonio Bailo, proprietor of a bookshop at Ro. 4, Calle de Carritas.

Bailo's wife Goya had painted about 1805. Her portrait, now in the National Gallery, Washington, D. C., is a beautifully simple, rather somber study of a middle-class woman of character and personality, as proud and self-confident as a queen. There is nothing in it of the smug vulgarity with which Goya depicted other members of the bourgeoisie, such as Javier's mother- and father-in-law. One can imagine that Señora Bailo had a good deal to say in choosing the books her husband would offer for sale or publish.

Bailo testified that in private conversations Goya spoke warmly of how he hated the French invaders. Others reported that Goya had actually left Madrid in an attempt to escape into unoccupied Spain, but had been forced to return by the threats of Joseph's Minister of Police.

On May 21, the commission recommended to King Ferdinand that he pardon the painter. When Ferdinand first received Goya, he is said to have told him: "You are a traitor, and you deserve to be exiled, if not garroted. But you are a great artist and we forgive you." Ferdinand knew he needed Goya and would need him more as time went on. Goya resumed his official duties as First Court Painter.

Ferdinand VII was one of the worst kings ever to rule

anywhere, and by far the worst of all monarchs of Spain. Utterly corrupt, utterly reactionary, and utterly stupid, he plunged Spain into moral, spiritual, and financial bankruptcy. Brigandage thrived and made travel virtually impossible. Strict censorship was imposed on every form of expression. The Inquisition was restored. Justice became a farce, as spying and informing turned the country into a police state. Under the rule of this absolute dictator Spain lost her colonies in Central and South America; even Florida went to the United States.

Restored to favor, but not readmitted to the royal entourage, Goya painted at least seven portraits of this degenerate sovereign—in his coronation robes, on horseback, in military uniform. If Goya thought it in his best interests to serve Ferdinand, he at least did not disguise his low estimate of Ferdinand's character. The costumes and the backgrounds of the portraits are all that even suggest majesty. The king himself is posed like a deformed doll crudely carved from wood by some primitive toymaker. His features speak only of cruelty, bigotry, and sensuality. The fact that Ferdinand allowed Goya to repeat these caricatures is indication enough of the king's conceit and lack of perception.

But Goya had other work with which to amuse himself. By October 28, 1816, he had completed a series of thirty-three etchings on the art of bullfighting, which he announced for sale in the *Diario de Madrid* and the *Gazeta* on that day. They could be bought singly or in sets at a printshop on the Calle Mayor. Seven more etchings were added for later editions, and four more really belong to the set.

The series, called the *Tauromaquia*, is almost a scholarly work on the history of this ritualistic sport. It begins with the origins of bullfighting among the Moors in Spain,

King Ferdinand VII of Spain. *Prado Museum, Madrid.*

221

Pedro Romero Kills a Bull, Plate 30 of Goya's *La Tauromaquia*.

continues through the period when bullfighting was reserved for the nobility, and records Goya's contemporary *toreros* and events Goya himself probably saw in the ring.

Like the *Caprichos* these prints are etching and aquatint, but their design is simpler and there is less of the storyteller in their conception than in the earlier series. Their most remarkable quality is the abstraction Goya has made of the nature and the action of the bulls. For the animals are the protagonists of the scenes; the men, even when depicted in their astonishing feats of agility and daring, are secondary.

Goya's observation has transcended that of the human eye, even that of the fastest camera. At first glance, the

222

spectator may think Goya's bulls do not appear real. Their positions and movements seem impossible, like caricatures. Gradually it becomes clear that Goya's observation is super-humanly accurate. The bulls—and the fighters too—do move as he perceived them. Here is the essence of the bull-fight—the fiction that is truer than truth.

The *Tauromaquia* had not occupied all of Goya's time. While working on the series during 1815, he also produced two of his best portraits: the one of Miguel Fernández y Flores, who was made Bishop of Marcopolis in that year, is in the Art Museum of Worcester, Massachusetts; the other, of Ignacio Omulryan y Rouera, Minister of the Council of the Indies, is in the Nelson Gallery, Kansas City, Missouri.

Both of them show that Goya had been studying El Greco. They are strongly expressionistic of Goya's feelings about the sitters, especially the portrait of Omulryan, in which Goya, himself growing old, seems very tender in depicting this aged man.

And, perhaps to relax, Goya again painted his grandson Mariano. He had done a delightful portrait of the blond child when Mariano was hardly able to stand up. Now, at the age of eight, the boy wears a *bolivar* hat, such as Goya himself wore. He is listening to music—perhaps one of the Spanish songs poor deaf Goya loved and may even have been croaking to the child to amuse him. The boy's elegant costume, like that of Javier in his wedding portrait, shows how proud Goya was that his descendants had risen above the laboring class to which José Goya had belonged. Mariano eventually bought himself a title.

Goya began another series of etchings, probably in 1816, after the *Tauromaquia* had been put on sale. They were not finished until about 1824. Goya never published them, a strange omission for so economical a man, especially

"Strange folly," Plate 3 of Goya's *Proverbs*.

since he had engraved them on expensive copper plates
ordered from England. These Goya stored with Javier
when he left Spain. The etchings were issued only in 1864,
by the Academy, which gave them the title *Proverbios*
("Proverbs"). In 1918, the Goya scholar Aureliano de
Beruete y Moret listed them in his catalogue of Goya's
works as *Disparates*, meaning stupidities or follies. This
title has a tone that implies Goya is pitying nonsense, probably not the case.

Spain has many proverbs, as any reader of *Don Quixote*
quickly becomes aware. Some of Goya's plates can be
matched with certain of the better known proverbs. Number 3, possibly the most famous of the series, apparently

illustrates the *refrano* (popular saying) "to go among the branches," meaning to talk through one's hat. Or it may mean "education in the higher branches," for no refuge is to be found in a dead tree.

Plate 21, perhaps the greatest work of art of them all, shows four Orientals—possibly rabbis or high priests—confronting an expressionistic elephant with a great book and with a string of bells. The elephant may signify the power of the mass of the people, who can be wheedled into accepting laws that will only repress them. Or the etching may illustrate the proverb: "Who will bell the cat?"

Goya seems to have twisted the common meanings by giving the scenes some special social or political or religious significance. No one now knows what any of these enigmatic etchings truly mean. They seem to be a second

"Animal folly," Plate 21 of Goya's *Proverbs*.

series of *Caprichos,* something Goya apparently had in mind when making the many drawings of the fantastic and absurd he did at this period of his life.

Like the second section of the *Caprichos,* many of the *Proverbs* are metaphors for the images in Goya's unconscious, which he himself probably did not understand. Some of them had occurred before in Goya's work, such as the phantom in Plate 2, which is like the "Bogeyman" of Plates 3 and 52 of the *Caprichos.*

Others seem to be travesties of Goya's own work. Plate 1 parodies the tapestry cartoon, *El Pelele* ("The Straw Man"), in which dainty girls are tossing a puppet in a blanket. In *Proverbs* 1 imbecilic or even insane women are trying to toss a man on whom is lying a donkey. *Proverbs* 6 is reminiscent of *The Disasters of War,* but here the figures are clearly insane. The unhappily wed couple of *Caprichos* 75 have become an androgynous monster in *Proverbs* 7. The game of the cartoon *Blindman's Buff (La Galina Ciega)* is turned into ghoulish rigadoon in *Proverbs* 12.

Proverbs 13 shows five men flying with the aid of the wings of some batlike bird. They are like Leonardo da Vinci's drawings of his projected flying machine. These figures reappear in Goya's fantastic *City on a Rock,* in New York's Metropolitan Museum of Art. Here, too, is the tower of reason of *The Dream of Lies and Inconstancy.* Beneath it, in the painting, a battle is in progress, and a city of the plains, in flames. The weird flying men hover in the clear blue sky as if to say that reason can elevate man above nonsensical destruction.

The etchings of the *Proverbs* are somber in tone. Often the aquatint is so dark as to obscure the forms, perhaps suggesting the obscurity of their meaning. Sinister and mysterious, Goya may be saying, are the labyrinthine ways of man's mind. When glimpsed through these ugly corridors, man's aspirations are nonsensical.

Paradoxically, Goya could emerge from this brooding to paint, in 1817, the cheerful *Saints Justa and Rufina* for the Cathedral of Seville. The two patron saints of that city are represented with all their attributes, and against the skyline of Seville. They are, however, plainly women of the streets, as Goya is said freely to have acknowledged. He told Ceán Bermúdez that he wanted "to make vice attractive and make them worship it."

Goya made the long journey to Seville to deliver the painting in person, and stayed with the painter José María Arango. He painted his host's son in gratitude for the hospitality.

City on a Rock. *The Metropolitan Museum of Art, New York, H. O. Havemeyer Collection.*

Also about this time Goya fulfilled his last official commission, an enormous painting of the Royal Philippine Company, presided over by King Ferdinand VII. This company was the great monopoly of the Spanish colonial merchants—the very incarnation of upper-middle-class financial policy. The painting now hangs in the Museum of Castres, in southern France. The session takes place in a large room, lighted by a window on the right. On each side, in sharp perspective, sit spectators in semidarkness; in the rear, on a dais, are the directors. The perspective and the uneven lighting give the picture great depth. Painted in blacks and grays, lightened by patches of color here and there, it is a masterpiece of interior painting.

In February, 1819, Goya moved out of Madrid to a villa he had bought on the west bank of the Manzanares River, near the Segovia Bridge and the meadow of San Isidro. From this house Goya had a view of Madrid and the Guadarrama Mountains, and there was good hunting on its sixty-five acres of land. The villa was known to the neighbors as *La Quinta del Sordo,* "the House of the Deaf Man." It became the rendezvous of Goya's old friends who were still alive and had not fled from Spain for political reasons: Ceán Bermúdez; and the painters Antonio Carnicero, Ascensio Julia, and José del Castillo. The Court was no longer Goya's dish.

To take care of him, Goya invited a distant cousin, Leocadia Zorilla Weiss, to live at the *Quinta.* Leocadia had had a husband, Isidro, of German extraction, a businessman in Madrid. He had initiated legal proceedings against her for misconduct as early as 1812, and had left her. Leocadia had a quarrelsome and an obstinate temper, as Goya's portrait of her shows, but she had two children—Guillermo and the five-year-old Maria del Rosario—and to Goya they made up for her bad disposition. Rosario may have been

Goya's child. He adored and idealized her. As for Leocadia, he could not hear her tirades, and could turn his head away from her sign language. He seems to have enjoyed the new arrangement.

In May, 1819, the Scolope Fathers of Madrid asked Goya to paint an altarpiece for their newly constructed Church of St. Anthony Abbot, in the Calle Hortaleza. He chose for a subject the last communion of their founder, St. Joseph of Calasanza.

St. Joseph (1556–1648) thought that the poverty of the common people was the basic cause of their sins. Their degradation he saw as the result of ignorance and neglect. Hence he founded schools with, for his day, advanced educational theories. A teacher, St. Joseph believed, not only must know what he is teaching, he must know how best to teach it. Goya had attended one of these schools

The Last Communion of St. Joseph of Calasanza. *St. Anthony Abbot, Madrid.*

PHOTO MAS, BARCELONA

sixty years before in Zaragoza. The subject appealed to
him for that reason and because St. Joseph had been, like
Goya himself, a simple Aragonese peasant.

The altarpiece is one of the very few of Goya's religious
works in which there is a true feeling of reverence. The
saint was old, as Goya himself was. The painter, so disillusioned with life as he had known it, transfers perhaps
his own longing for spiritual peace and acceptance into
the kneeling figure bathed in a weak golden light. Around
the saint, in Rembrandtesque chiaroscuro, are a group of
men and a group of boys, their faces repeating the ecstasy
of the rugged St. Joseph as he receives the mystical sacrament. It is said that an ignorant water carrier—one of the
seven-hundred-odd who practiced this dignified trade in
Madrid then—chanced to see the work in Goya's studio
and fell on his knees before the easel as if it were an altar.

For good measure, though he was apparently again in
financial need, Goya gave the Fathers an *Agony in the
Garden*. This, too, is deeply sincere. The praying Christ
is like the victim of *The Third of May, 1808* and of the
first *Capricho*. He, too, is a peasant type, not the ascetic
Savior so common in the work of other Spanish painters.
Goya is expressing not only the spiritual torture of the
Son of God, but his own mental torture and that of the
oppressed sons of the Spanish earth.

Like these paintings for the Scolope Fathers is the
deeply emotional *Repentant St. Peter*, now in the Phillips
Memorial Gallery, Washington, D. C. Painted at approximately the same time, it is even more advanced in insight
and technique than the *St. Joseph* and the *Agony in the
Garden*. The free brushwork, the luminosity of the pre-
dominantly green coloring, the monumental bulk of the
figure anticipate the impressionism of Cézanne. Psychologically it could be a self-portrait of Goya, so keenly felt is
the spiritual agony of the disciple who denied his Lord.

The Repentant St. Peter. *The Phillips Collection, Washington, D.C.*

The painting is another example of Goya's theory that in nature there are only masses of light or of shadow, planes that advance or recede, reliefs or backgrounds.

Before the year 1819 was out, Goya was seriously ill again. His "acute and dangerous illness," as he called it, may have been diphtheria. He seems to have indulged in deep self-pity, for the double portrait he made of himself and his doctor, Eugenio García Arrieta, in 1820, shows Goya as about the sickest creature who ever survived. One version of the portrait is in the Minneapolis Institute of Arts. The shadowy figures in the background—a priest and perhaps a figure of Death—show how near Goya thought his end was and how his mind was still haunted by the phantoms which swarm in the dim regions just beyond consciousness.

231

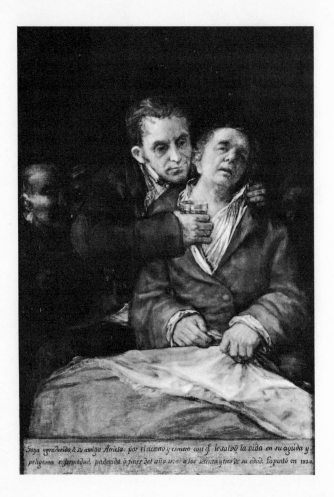

Goya and Dr. Arrieta.
The Minneapolis Institute of Arts.

As in the work Goya produced after his previous critical
illness in 1792, these visions of another world demanded
expression. It is as if Goya, like the skeleton of *The Disasters,* had to report on the underworld he had explored.
He began covering the walls of his villa with the symbols
of this realm of loneliness and death and shadows. (The
paintings, done in oil directly on the plaster of the walls,
were transferred to canvas by Salvador Martínez Cabrels
and removed to the Prado in 1881. They now are arranged
there as they were in Goya's *Quinta.*)

232

These are Goya's *pinturas negras* ("black paintings"), so-called because they seem devoid of the colors of light, and to have been executed only in black and white. Terrifyingly somber, wild and mocking, they burn—for once one's eyes grow used to their darkness, greens and golds and warm browns and reds appear—with the baleful glow of an old fire whose light illumines only shadows. Decay and death, ugliness and evil, Goya is saying in them, devour youth and innocence and hope.

Like the bloodthirsty *Judith* with her dripping knife opposite the entrance to the high-ceilinged, rectangular dining room on the ground floor, every seductress slays her lover as he sleeps. The gay young lovers who go out in the morning to picnic in San Isidro's meadow return in the dusk as old and blind and reeling drunkards. Death begs for a sip of the soup a leering old man is spooning into his

Witches' Sabbath, from the Quinta del Sordo. *Prado Museum, Madrid.*

toothless mouth. Hideous hags—obscene witches all—listen in darkness to the preachments of a cassocked, he-goat Satan. And at the end of the room an age-wasted Saturn, eyes bulging with greed, devours the tiny, well-formed man he squeezes in his gaunt hands. Time, the ogre with slavering jaws, crunches the bones of man's endeavors and for memorials spits out a few bloody gobbets not even Time can swallow.

Above the dining room, where Goya's friends would gather, a lonely dog howls against a vast empty darkened sky. Such is man's plea to be heard in the desert of the world. Two men half-sunk in quicksand savagely cudgel each other to death; hatred survives in man up to his last gasp. Fantastic and loathsome figures—witches? Fates?—float through a dark, cloudy sky, casting the sinister shadow of evil over man's best-laid plans.

What is most fearful about the "black paintings" is the ease with which Goya seems to move among the phantoms. The broad, sweeping, vigorous technique with which he executed them is the same, only more so, as that he used for the subjects of this world with which he was most familiar. Everything is expression on the House of the Deaf Man's walls, nothing is representation. Here are howls of disillusionment, sighs of loneliness and disappointment, cackling laughter of scornful ridicule. The feeling is too strong to be expressed in an articulate statement. Finally, the spectator howls in response, shocked beyond thought by this revelation of a world he suspects may be the real one. Of *The Disasters* Goya said: "This I saw." In the "black paintings" he is saying: "This I know."

In this same period of despondency, which lasted roughly from 1819 to 1824, Goya was trying to preserve his faith. It had been sorely tried, not only by illness and loneliness, but by the increasingly reactionary trend of

Ferdinand VII's policies. Another expression of it is a cycle of drawings that seem dedicated to the ideals of Truth and Freedom. An artist's drawings constitute his private diary; Goya's show that however much he may have compromised with officialdom, in conscience he identified himself with the fighters for liberty in many countries, not Spain alone. His was the conscience of the modern man.

Over seven hundred of Goya's drawings are still extant. Many have been lost. The subjects range from sketches of everyday life, like those of the Sanlúcar album, to fantasies and symbols. One, for example, entitled "He Does Not Know What He Is Doing," shows a broken statue, symbolizing Liberty, smashed in an orgy of reaction. In another, a man feeds his own severed head with a spoon, while another man pours liquid through a funnel into the stump of a neck. Here is a symbol of the mechanical way pedants acquire lifeless knowledge.

Several drawings show the results of Napoleon's im-

The Return from San Isidro, from the Quinta del Sordo. *Prado Museum, Madrid.*

235

petuous dissolution of the convents and monasteries, which forced nuns and monks abruptly into a world with which they had not been trained to cope. In this group Goya is at times humane and pitying; at others, satirical. There are other drawings condemning cruel and unjust punishments, and many that extol the dignity of human work. A few are frankly Rabelaisian. Many others are examples of Goya's highly original, enigmatic imagery, suggesting far more than they depict.

Goya's drawings rank with those of the greatest artists. Possibly their most remarkable characteristic is their ability to suggest by a sepia wash a whole range of color. They are free from any of the restrictions an accurate rendering of nature requires; they are broad impressions and expressions given form by the simplest, most economical means possible. Full of warm dramatic feeling, they have great abstract power.

Saturn, from the Quinta del Sordo.
Prado Museum, Madrid.
PHOTO MAS, BARCELONA

The Water Carrier.
Museum, Budapest.

Peasant Carrying a Woman, brush drawing with brown washes. *Courtesy of the Hispanic Society of America, New York.*

Goya's confidence in, and respect for, the workingman also appears in a series of paintings he did of common laborers: *The Knife Grinder* and *The Water Carrier,* in the Budapest Museum of Fine Arts; and the magnificent *The Forge,* in the Frick Collection, New York City. The last is a large canvas executed in grays and blacks, except for the red glow of the forge itself, and with broad, vigorous brushstrokes. The powerful anatomy of its three figures is distorted to express their furious energy. Everything is concentrated on action; there are no distracting details. The tremendous muscular thrust of the man with the raised hammer is an effect Goya loved to reproduce; it appears also in "Peasant Carrying a Woman" and "Torture of a Man"—two wash drawings in the Hispanic Society of America, New York City.

Also during this period of introspection Goya made a series of three etchings dealing with prisoners. Several wash drawings preceded them, on which Goya made ironic notes, such as: "Guilty of descent from the Jews," "Guilty of wagging their tongues in a different way," "Guilty of being born differently." The captions of the etchings read: "You ought to be able to hold a prisoner without needing to torture him"; "The punishment is as barbarous as the crime"; "Why don't you execute him at once if he is guilty?" They are monumental designs in spite of their small (average four by three inches) format, and forcefully express a deep humanitarian feeling.

Torture was widespread as a legal weapon of both secular justice and the Inquisition. It was, of course, abhorrent to the eighteenth-century rationalists. The great reformer, the Benedictine monk Benito Jeronimo Feijoo (1676–1764), had tried to defeat it; and Jovellanos also tried to have it abolished, though in his capacity as a judge he was compelled to use it. The *Prisoners* are Goya's private pro-

The Forge. *Copyright The Frick Collection, New York.*

239

test against this aspect of man's inhumanity to man; they were not published during his lifetime, for he may also have intended them symbolically—the spirit of Spain imprisoned and tortured by reactionary absolutism.

Goya's portraits during this same period also show his forthright admiration of democracy. The most striking is the simple but forceful portrait (1820) of his trusted friend Don Tiburcio Pérez in New York City's Metropolitan Museum of Art. The architect poses in his shirtsleeves, in a free, easy attitude far removed from the artificial attitudes of Goya's portraits of Court people. Pérez' costume is wholly black and white, as was typical of Goya's style at that time—anything to simplify so that only the spiritualized human image would attract the spectator's eye. Goya's blacks and white, however, are never solid and dull. They are composed of countless hues applied in little, separated brushstrokes that do not even form planes of color.

Another portrait, similar in its direct, powerful, flowing treatment, is the one of Pérez' uncle, Don Juan Antonio Cuervo (1819), now in the Cleveland Museum of Art. Cuervo, also an architect, was made Director of the Academy of San Fernando in 1815.

For all of Ferdinand VII's brutal repression of liberalism, insurrection after insurrection during the six years of his absolute rule had racked the country. Finally, in Cádiz, the cradle of Spanish liberties, General Rafael del Riego y Núñez arose as the man the liberals needed to lead them. When an ill-paid, ill-equipped Spanish army was embarking there in January, 1820, to suppress the colonial revolutions in South America, Riego induced them to mutiny. The parliament supported the revolutionaries. Ferdinand was forced to accept the constitution he had suppressed in 1814. Riego, the hero of the times, kept Ferdinand a prisoner in Cádiz.

Don Tiburcio Perez. *The Metropolitan Museum of Art, New York,*
Theodore M. Davis Collection.

241

On April 4, 1820, a meeting of the Academy was called so that its members might swear allegiance to the constitution. Goya took the oath. He celebrated the long-awaited event with a drawing that shows a young woman whipping off the bats of reaction. "Divine Reason," says the caption, "spares none of them." Goya was rejoicing that at last Reason had triumphed.

His joy was short-lived. The liberals had no experience in governing. Friction between them and the absolutists culminated in a bloody clash in Madrid in July, 1822. The Royalists, supported by the seventy thousand of the clergy whom the constitution had thrown out of work, formed a government and negotiated with Louis XVIII of France. King Louis, seeing the danger of the liberal revolution to his own throne, and to that of all other countries, got the Holy Alliance to send an army to rescue his cousin Ferdinand from captivity in Cádiz. It arrived in May, 1823.

Thanks to these troops, by August, 1823, Ferdinand was free to rule in more absolute power than ever. His reprisals on all liberals were terrible. At least forty thousand Constitutionalists were imprisoned before he was through. Many of them were tortured into informing against others. Suspects were lynched, or hanged by drumhead courts. The universities were purged of liberal influences. All army men and civil servants had to swear that they belonged to no secret societies.

Goya's liberal leanings were well known. He determined to remain at liberty. On September 17, 1823, he made over the *Quinta* to his grandson Mariano, and went into hiding until the first frenzy might be over. He took refuge with Don José Duaso y Latre, a learned Aragonese canon, one of the first Spanish mountain climbers, and editor of the *Gazeta*. Don José's house sheltered many of his liberal friends, and Goya stayed there for three months.

Doña María Martínez de Puga. *Copyright The Frick Collection,
New York.*

243

Leocadia Weiss had already fled to France with Rosario, for her son Guillermo was now proscribed as a national militiaman. Goya, old and alone, determined to follow her, if not perhaps for her society, then for the company of Rosario and the comfort both could give him.

As First Court Painter, Goya had to apply to Ferdinand VII for permission to leave Spain "to take the mineral waters of Plombières, in France, in order to help his rheumatism." Ferdinand probably saw through this pretext, but he also saw that granting the request was an easy way of getting rid of the old man and his dangerous propaganda. On May 30, 1824, the king granted Goya permission to be absent for six months.

Goya's farewell to Spain was the portrait of Doña María Martínez de Puga, which now hangs in the Frick Collection, New York City. It is a bold, utterly simple portrait of a woman of the middle class, rendered with broad, slashing brushstrokes that give it a sensation of actual life. The yellow hair ribbon, the gold earrings and watch, and the pale flesh tones set off the blacks of the gown and the blue-grays of the background as if to tell the spectator that this quiet, reserved woman could flash with wit and feminine authority. The technique is new for Goya. Even at his advanced age and in a time of personal crisis he wished to keep on experimenting as he had done throughout his life.

General Riego, the leader of the liberals, had been captured by the French and handed over to the royal authorities. He was tried as a traitor and convicted. On November 7, 1823, he was executed. Doña María is said to have been his wife. The "Hymn of Riego," the song of the revolutionaries, and Goya's portrait, still keep alive his memory and man's invincible quest for self-respect and freedom.

11

Still Learning

Goya had small intention of taking any cure at the waters of Plombières in northeastern France. Instead, he headed straight for Bordeaux, in southwestern France, where many Spanish exiles were living. It would be cure enough for his troubled soul just to get out of a Spain that had relapsed into greater defiance of Reason than ever. Once across the Pyrenees he could breathe in freedom and in safety and in dignity.

Nor did he have much intention of staying long in Bordeaux; not, at least, until he had seen Paris. The long, hard journey from Madrid had not sapped his prodigious energy. After three days, not of rest but of dining out "as though he were a young student," he was off to the capital.

A letter written on June 27, 1824, by Goya's old friend Leandro Fernández de Moratín further describes the painter's first visit to Bordeaux: "Goya actually arrived, deaf, old, stupid, and feeble, and without knowing a word of French, and without bringing a servant . . . and so pleased and so eager to see everything. . . . He should not go out except in a carriage, but I do not know if he will agree. . . . We shall see later whether this journey [to Paris] will leave him still alive. . . ."

Moratín (1760–1828), though fourteen years younger than Goya, was apparently envious of his friend's energy and enthusiasm. He himself appears old and fat in the portrait Goya made of him in 1824. A playwright who modeled his works after Molière, Moratín had left Spain in 1821 out of disgust at Ferdinand VII's repression of liberties. He was now teaching school in Bordeaux, and was the leader of the Spanish intellectuals who had settled there.

Goya's journey to Paris certainly left him alive. Moratín had recommended him to a mutual friend, Arnao. Arnao found lodgings for Goya, who had arrived by July 8, and promised to send him back to mother-hen Moratín by September.

The seventy-eight-year-young traveler apparently had the time of his life in the metropolis, which made Madrid seem like a provincial town. A drawing Goya made of himself then humorously shows his enjoyment. He visited the Salon, where Géricault was exhibiting his *Raft of the Medusa* [1] and Delacroix, his *Massacre at Chios*. To Goya, however, these Romantics were saying nothing new. He himself had anticipated them. It would be another fifty years before Courbet and Manet would discover and be influenced by Goya.

Horace Vernet, whom Goya met in Paris, and Jean Auguste Dominique Ingres were also exhibiting at the Salon. Goya thus could observe the transition from the Classical to the Romantic School of painting in this capital of the art world. Ingres' tight portraits of the bourgeoisie of the Restoration Period in France Goya would have scorned as being done in a style he himself had long since set aside.

[1] The shipwreck of the *Medusa* off the coast of Senegal in 1819 horrified the world of that time as the sinking of the *Titanic* did the world of 1912. Goya painted an impression of the disaster in 1819. His *The Second of May, 1808*, painted in 1814, was ten years ahead of Delacroix's style. His two small paintings, also of 1819, of the murder by Iroquois Indians of Jean de Brébeuf, Archbishop of Quebec, in 1649, show Goya's romantic treatment of a brutal incident in history.

There was nothing, in fact, that Goya thought worth taking away from Paris with him. He made two portraits of his Spanish hosts, the Ferrers, and a painting of a picador attacking a bull, as well as some line drawings of bullfights done from memory. He brought Spain to France. Smugly he returned to Bordeaux, having settled the financial matters that had really taken him to Paris in the first place.

In June Goya had stayed at the school run by Manuel Silvela, who had been Mayor of Madrid, for the sons of the Spanish émigrés of Bordeaux. Leocadia Weiss and Rosario were boarders and in straitened circumstances; Guillermo Weiss was in Bergerac with the refugee citizen-army. Goya wanted to reunite his household, and so took a house for all of them at 24 (now 38), Cours de Tournay. But he was restless; he moved to two other houses in the next three years: 10, Rue de la Croix Blanche; and 39 (now 57), Cours de l'Indépendence, owned by Pio de Molina. According to Moratín, Goya and Leocadia quarreled frequently.

At first Goya clung to Moratín, who reported: "This Goya goes along with me everywhere, and does not leave me one free moment." Yet Moratín liked his own solicitous role for the man he must have realized was greater than he. The playwright's works have been forgotten by all but specialists, with the possible exception of *El Sí de las Niñas* (*How Girls Say Yes*). At this time he was trying to finish a history of the Spanish stage.

Gradually, as Goya got used to his new environment, he became more independent. There was the chocolate shop of Branlio Poc, a Zaragozan, in the Rue de la Petite Taupe (now Rue de la Huguerie), where he could meet other members of the Spanish colony who gathered for *tertulias* and to sip their national drink. Spanish chocolate was a composition of cocoa, sugar, and cinnamon pressed into cakes that were then dissolved in hot water and stirred till frothy. A cup of this brew was preceded by a drink of cold water sweetened with colored sugar, and followed by another. For hours they would play a game of connecting with lines five arbitrarily placed dots so as to make a recognizable human figure.

His chief companion was a young painter of marine scenes, Antonio de Brugado, in whose progress Goya took great interest. The two would go walking together, Goya hating the infirmity that now made him need a stick, and pleading with his young friend not to use sign language so obviously as to attract attention to Goya's deafness. He took up music again, and would strum old songs on a guitar. But when he asked Brugado to sing for him, Goya could only shake his head, pathetically murmuring *"Nada, nada,"* for he could not hear a single note. He was to bequeath his palette to Brugado.

Rosario, or Mariquita, as the French called her, was all his joy. Determined that she should learn to paint, and blinded by his affection to her singular lack of talent, he apprenticed her first to a designer of wallpaper named Vernet, and then to Antoine Lacour, son of the Director of the Bordeaux Museum.

Goya had little use for the kind of instruction Rosario was getting. When he visited Lacour's studio and saw the work on the students' easels, he would mutter: "That's not it, that's not the way."

Goya, however, neglected to provide for Rosario in his will. She later became a copyist, and also was the drawing instructor of Queen Isabella II. She died on July 31, 1840, of a fever caused by her panic at being caught in a riot in Madrid.

Rosario wanted to paint miniatures, and so nothing

would do but that Goya, forever a child, learn that skill too. He got himself some round pieces of ivory, and, in 1825, after a winter of experimenting, wrote to a friend in Paris: "I have a collection of about forty examples, but it is a type of original miniature that I have never seen before, resembling the brushwork of Velázquez rather than that of Mengs." Goya's method was to blacken the ivory, then let a drop of water fall on it. This he would spread, erasing the black and uncovering the white ground on which he would trace highlights.

Two of these miniatures—*Old Man Looking for Fleas* and *Woman with a Blowing Skirt*—are in a private collection in New York City. They are the most unusual ones in the whole history of that form, painted broadly and with no attention to the detail that characterizes most miniatures. The first, two and a half inches square, has all the visionary quality of the sixteen-foot-long black paintings. The second, three and a half inches square, has the monumental quality of a fresco. Here is a grand, fantastic expressionism at a peak not to be reached again in art for another forty years. Goya was still learning—and mastering.

He also returned to lithography, a technique he had first attempted in 1819, when his friend José Cardano had brought from Paris to Madrid examples of the newly discovered process. Lithography had been invented by a twenty-five-year-old Munich author, Aloys Senefelder, in order that he might economically reproduce his own unpublished works. Intended as a substitute for letterpress, it was immediately put to use for the printing of music, by which Senefelder made the fortune his literary efforts failed to bring him. By 1816 the process had been perfected by Godefredo Engelman, an Alsatian of Mulhouse, in his shop in Paris. Goya, the first major artist to use the technique, made eighteen lithographs in all.

In lithography the artist draws with greasy ink or crayon on a stone porous enough to absorb grease and water. After he has created his design, he sponges the stone with a weak acid that cleans the pores in the unworked areas. A gum solution is then spread over the whole stone. This forms a protective skin over the unworked areas, but does not stick to the greasy design. The stone is then cleaned with water, which sinks in except on the greasy areas, and is kept damp during the printing. An inked roller passed over the plate picks up the greasy design. Damp paper laid on the stone and put through a press reproduces the design, giving effects unobtainable by any other process.

In Bordeaux Goya worked directly on the stone, as if he had no time to waste on transfers. His eyes were failing, and he had been ill again in the spring of 1825—almost to the point of death, as Moratín reported on June 16. He had to use a magnifying glass, and carry the stone from worktable to window to truly see what he had done. On December 20, 1825, he wrote his friend Joaquín Ferrer in Paris: "I have neither sight nor pulse, nor pen nor inkpot. I lack everything. It is only my will which I have to excess."

That will produced four nostalgic lithographs of bull-fighting, which Goya published early in 1826, through the printshop of Gaulon, as *The Bulls of Bordeaux*. Ferrer, to whom Goya had sent a sample of the series to be marketed, tried to get Goya to bring out a new edition of the twenty-year-old *Caprichos* instead. Goya would have none of that. "I have better prizes today which should sell better," the octogenarian replied with the cocky assurance of his youth. *The Bulls of Bordeaux*, however, attracted few purchasers, even though, according to their creator, the price was "modest."

In these lithographs, as always now with Goya, the subject matter is reduced to the purest essence. Everything in them is simplified to an emphatic statement—the tension of a small, slight man versus an enormously powerful bull. The spectator senses the same suspense he would experience in the amphitheater itself. The huddled crowds in the ring express the tension of a situation that at any moment may erupt into disaster.

This charged atmosphere Goya captures in an extraordinary range of tones that, though only blacks and whites, suggest hectic colors. The lines are free. A minimum of definition opens up endless meanings. There is irony and satire, as in Number Three, in which the spectators are laughing at a gored picador. To this one Ceán Bermúdez added the bitter comment: "This is the voice of the rational, religious, enlightened public of Spain."

The Bulls of Bordeaux are among the most poetic of Goya's works. All are re-creations of scenes which once his eye saw clearly and over which his mind played long and

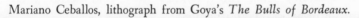

Mariano Ceballos, lithograph from Goya's *The Bulls of Bordeaux*.

deeply. The lithograph of Mariano Ceballos, for example, records an experience of over forty years before, when the celebrated bullfighter had come from South America to astonish Spain with his intrepidity. The plates are the voice of an emotion that has been recollected in tranquility.

Goya had adjusted himself to life in exile. He savored the air of Bordeaux as it blew fresh from the water and sweetened with the enlightened ideals of France. He took an interest in almost every facet of the life of the city, visiting the fairs and the circus with Leocadia and Rosario, treating the indigent among the émigrés to *puchero* (stew). Everything had interest for him—the street life, the mountebanks, the workmen, a man being guillotined. He drew them all. The dead animals and birds in the market stalls seemed to fascinate him. These he painted in a series of still lifes—hares, woodcocks, ducks—which are in a private collection in New York City. Dead though the subjects clearly are, the vitality Goya gave their forms makes the spectator sense the quickness they had before their springs of action were uncoiled.

Moratín wrote that Goya loved Bordeaux, "its surrounding country, its climate, the food, and the independence and quiet he enjoys there." Yet Goya worried about his investments, which he had entrusted to Santiago Galos, a French businessman and banker of Bordeaux, in whom he had great confidence. Goya wrote often to Javier about the inheritance he was putting in order for his son and grandson. And he hankered after Madrid.

His original six months' leave had long since expired. Goya got it extended by mail on the pretext that he wanted to take the waters at Bagnères—something he had no intention of doing. In May, 1826, he determined to take the long, racking journey—to see the city of his triumphs and his disappointments, to get his leave of absence extended

Portrait of Goya, 1826,
by Vicente Lopez.
Prado Museum, Madrid.
PHOTO MAS, BARCELONA

indefinitely, to attend to his finances. He seemed to be afraid that he might, like Titian, live to be ninety-nine and be dependent on others after he could no longer paint.

He had an interview with Ferdinand VII. The king extended Goya's leave indefinitely and guaranteed him a salary for the rest of his life on the condition that Goya sit for a portrait by Vicente López y Portaña, of Valencia, then as fashionable a painter in the capital as Goya himself had been. The portrait is professional but rather uninspired. Goya, the story goes, got tired of López' slow, painstaking procedures, and commanded him to stop when Goya himself could see that the portrait was done. The important part of the painting, aside from being apparently

253

a good likeness of Goya near the close of his life, is the accurate reproduction of Goya's palette (see page 95).

Goya revisited the *Quinta* to see its walls he had covered with his dreary visions, and San Antonio de la Florida, to see its dome which he had covered with his bright and exuberant ones. The rest of Madrid held nothing for him, gripped as it was in the ever-tightening vise of King Ferdinand's ruthless absolutism. Bordeaux, much as Goya pretended it did not suit him, he realized was a happier habitat.

Mariano went back with his grandfather, for everyone seemed to fear that the old man would be "left dead in the corner of some inn." They arrived in early July, 1826, somewhat to the astonishment of the oversolicitous Moratín, who had doubted he would ever see Goya alive again.

Goya went on painting portraits of his friends: Galos, now in the Barnes Foundation, Merion, Pennsylvania; Juan Bautista de Muguiro, a liberal refugee and also a banker and businessman; José Pio de Molino, a former mayor of Bordeaux—Goya's last work and unfinished. But his great tribute to his adopted city is the tenderly beguiling *Milkmaid of Bordeaux,* painted in 1827. Here the color he had abandoned for so many years in favor of blacks and whites and grays, he readopted with all the soft brightness of the early tapestry cartoons, but with a far livelier technique. The painting fairly vibrates owing to Goya's short, crossed brushstrokes. The milkmaid's name has long since been lost, but she lives as the epitome of the soft ways of southern France and of the grace of womanhood.

Goya made another brief journey to Spain in 1827, perhaps again to straighten out his finances, more probably just to see Javier and Mariano. By January, 1828, he was pleading with them to visit him in Bordeaux, offering to pay the cost of a subsequent trip to Paris for Mariano and

Gumersinda. Javier replied with many questions about the inheritances and with many excuses for not coming. Goya's anxiety that they might not make the trip so exhausted him that by March he was ill again. By the end of that month he wrote that he was "happy to be better, so as to welcome my dearly loved travelers."

At last Mariano and Gumersinda arrived on March 28. Goya was so overcome with joy at seeing them that he had to take to his bed again. "Please God, you can come to join them," he wrote to Javier in a shaky hand. On April 1, they had breakfast together. Early the next morning Goya awoke to find himself paralyzed on one side.

His mind remained clear, and he could speak, but only in a whisper, to ask when Javier would come. For two weeks he lingered, perhaps envisioning another astonishing production like those which in the past had always followed a serious illness.

Then, about two o'clock in the morning of April 16, 1828, Leocadia, who was watching by Goya's bedside, saw that he was awake. His eyes seemed to be focused on his hands, the hands that had wrought such marvels. Presently those eyes, which had seen so deeply into human beings and the things of this world, closed forever.

The next day, after a funeral service in the Church of Notre Dame, Goya was laid to rest in the tomb of his relative-by-marriage and friend, Martín Goicoechea, in the Cemetery of the Chartreuse in Bordeaux. Goicoechea had died three years before.

Fifty years later, Spain roused itself to reclaim one who had been among its greatest glories. But ten years more went by before the tomb at Bordeaux was opened on November 13, 1888. Then it was found that Goya's bones were mixed with those of his kinsman. But not inseparably. Goya's were those of a colossus, with a strong, arched spinal column and huge tibias. There was, however, only one skull, not Goya's. The tomb was sealed again.

It was not until May, 1900, that the remains were returned to Madrid. They were placed in the Church of San Isidro, beside those of Moratín. A monument to Goya was erected in the church.

Once again they were moved, through the efforts of the sculptor Mariano Benlliure. All that is mortal of Goya now lies under a plain stone slab with a simple inscription—name and dates—beneath the immortal frescoes of the ceiling of San Antonio de la Florida.

Chronology

1746   Francisco de Paula José Goya y Lucientes born in Fuendetodos, province of Aragon, Spain, March 30.

1749   Father moves to Zaragoza.

1758(?) First known painting—decoration of reliquary in Church of the Assumption, Fuendetodos.

1759   Enters studio of José Luzán, in Zaragoza. Later also a pupil of Juan Ramirez.

1763   Leaves Zaragoza for Madrid.

1766   Fails for third time in competition for a scholarship at the Royal Academy of Fine Arts of San Fernando.

1769   Arrives in Rome, early in year.

1771   Wins commendation in competition of Royal Academy of Fine Arts, Parma, June 27. Returns to Zaragoza, late summer. Awarded commission for frescoes in Cathedral of El Pilar, Zaragoza, October 21.

1773   Marries Josefa Bayeu y Subias, July 25.

1775   Returns to Madrid. Delivers sample tapestry cartoon, May 24. Commissioned to paint more tapestry cartoons, June 18.

1778   Executes eighteen etchings after Velázquez.

1779   Presented at Court, January 9.

1780 Elected to membership in Academy of San Fernando, July 7. Returns to Zaragoza to execute more frescoes in Cathedral of El Pilar.

1781 Quarrels with Francisco Bayeu and Committee on Art of the Cathedral, and returns to Madrid, May. Commissioned to paint altarpiece for Church of San Francisco el Grande, July 25 (not unveiled until November, 1784). Father dies, December 17.

1783 First important portrait commission—Count of Floridablanca—January 22. Visits Infante Don Luis de Borbón at Los Arenas and paints portraits of his family, late summer.

1784 Son Javier born, December 2, Goya's only child to reach maturity (died 1854).

1785 Portrait of the Duchess of Osuna. (Goya's friendship with the Osuna family and their patronage of him may have begun in 1783.)

1786 Begins second series of tapestry cartoons as official painter to Royal Tapestry Manufactory of Santa Barbara, June. Portrait of King Charles III in hunting costume.

1789 Appointed Court Painter to King Charles IV, April.

1793 Suffers severe illness, January–March, which leaves him totally deaf.

1794 Sends eleven easel paintings to the Academy, January 4, probably Goya's first works in his new expressionistic style (*The Madhouse, The Burial of the Sardine,* etc.) Exact dates of each of these paintings uncertain.

1795 Elected Director of the School of Painting of the Academy of San Fernando, October 4. Probable beginning of his relationship with the Duchess of Alba.

1796–7   Visits Duchess of Alba in Sanlúcar, October, remaining until the following March. Portrait of Duchess (the Hispanic Society of America) with cryptic inscription and two rings. Resigns as Director of Painting at Academy because of deafness.

1798   Frescoes in Church of San Antonio de la Florida, Madrid, August 1–December 20.

1799   *Los Caprichos* put on sale, February 6. Appointed First Court Painter to King Charles IV, October 31. Guest of the royal family at La Granja, autumn.

1800   Group portrait of the family of Charles IV, June.

1801   Guest of Prime Minister Manuel Godoy at Aranjuez, spring. Portrait of Godoy, October.

1805   Javier Goya marries Gumersinda Goicoechea y Galarza, July.

1807   Goya's only grandchild, Mariano, born (died 1874).

1808   Insurrection in Madrid; incidents of May 2 and 3. Goya visits Zaragoza, October, to record ruins caused by siege. Trapped in Fuendetodos by war against French invaders.

1810   *The Disasters of War* begun; finished about 1820. (Not published until 1863.)

1812   Josefa Goya dies, June 20. Portraits of Duke of Wellington, probably in August.

1814   Restoration of King Ferdinand VII, March. Goya paints *The Second of May, 1808* and *The Third of May, 1808*, spring. Goya's loyalty investigated, November 14. (Goya cleared, and granted amnesty by Ferdinand VII, May 21, 1815.)

1816   *Tauromaquia* put on sale, October 28. Goya

probably begins *Proverbs,* not finished until about 1824; published, 1864.

1819 Purchases *"Quinta del Sordo,"* February. First work in lithography. Seriously ill, autumn.

1820 "Black paintings" in *La Quinta del Sordo* (now in the Prado through gift of Baron Emil d'Erlanger). Swears allegiance to new constitutional regime, April 4.

1823 Constitution abolished by Ferdinand VII. Goya transfers *Quinta* to grandson, September 17. Goes into hiding.

1824 Goes into voluntary exile in Bordeaux, June. Visits Paris, July–September.

1826 *The Bulls of Bordeaux* published. Goya returns to Madrid, May–July, to get his leave of absence extended. Portrait painted by Vicente López.

1827 Revisits Madrid. *The Milkmaid of Bordeaux.* Paints last portrait (José Pio de Molina).

1828 Dies in Bordeaux, April 16.

Bibliography

Books

Adhémar, Jean. *Goya,* tr. by Denys Sutton and David Weston. New York: Continental Book Center, Inc., 1948.

Barbarrossa, Mercedes C. *The Living Goya.* Boston: Meador Publishing Co., 1939.

Beruete y Moret, Aureliano de. *Goya as a Portrait Painter,* tr. by Selwyn Brinton. Boston and New York: Houghton Mifflin Co., 1922.

Blanco Soler, Carlos. *Goya, su Enfermidad y su Arte.* Madrid: Bolanos y Aguilar, 1947.

Calvert, Albert F. *Goya—An Account of His Life and Works.* London: John Lane, The Bodley Head, 1908.

Casanova, Jacques. *The Memoirs of Jacques Casanova de Seingault,* tr. by Arthur Machen. 3 vols. New York: Dover Publications, Inc., 1961.

Cooper, Leonard. *The Age of Wellington.* New York: Dodd, Mead & Co., 1963.

Crow, John A. *Spain: The Root and the Flower.* New York, Evanston, and London: Harper & Row, Inc., 1963.

Davis, Curtis Carroll. *The King's Chevalier: A Biography of Lewis Littlepage.* Indianapolis and New York: The Bobbs-Merrill Co., Inc., 1961.

Derwent, Lord (G. H. Johnstone). *Goya, an Impression of Spain.* London: Methuen & Co., Ltd., 1930.

de Salas, Xavier. *Francisco José de Goya y Lucientes.* New York: Barnes & Noble, Inc., 1962.

Ezquerra del Bayo, Joaquin. *La Duquesa de Alba y Goya.* Madrid: Ruiz Hermanos, 1928.

Ferrari, Enrique L. *Goya: The Frescoes in San Antonio de la Florida in Madrid,* tr. by Stuart Gilbert. New York: Albert Skira, 1956.

Formaggio, Dino. *Goya.* New York: Thomas Yoseloff, 1961.

Gassier, Pierre. *Goya.* New York: Skira, Inc., 1955.

Goya y Lucientes, Francisco José. *The Complete Etchings of*

Goya. Foreword by Aldous Huxley. New York: Crown Publishers, 1943.

―――. *Epistolario . . . : Parentesis por Guillermo Diaz Plaja.* Barcelona: Editorial Mentora, 1928.

Gudiol y Ricart, José. *Goya.* New York: The Hyperion Press, 1941.

Harris, Tomás. *Goya: Engravings and Lithographs.* Oxford: Bruno Cassirer, 1964.

Holland, Vyvyan. *Goya, A Pictorial Biography.* New York: The Viking Press, Inc., 1961.

Kany, Charles E. *Life and Manners in Madrid, 1750–1800.* Berkeley: University of California Press, 1932.

Klingender, F. D. *Goya in the Democratic Tradition.* London: Sidgwick & Jackson, Ltd., 1948.

López-Rey, José. *A Cycle of Goya's Drawings.* New York: The Macmillan Co., 1956.

―――. *Goya's Caprichos: Beauty, Reason and Caricature.* Princeton: Princeton University Press, 1953.

―――. *On Goya's Legend and Life.* New York: Wildenstein & Co., 1950.

Malraux, André. *Saturn: An Essay on Goya.* New York: Phaidon Publishers, Inc., 1957.

Matheron, Laurent. *Goya.* Paris: Schulz et Thuillie, 1858.

Mayer, August L. *Francisco de Goya,* tr. by Robert West. London and Toronto: J. M. Dent & Sons, Ltd., 1924.

Moynihan, Rodrigo. *Goya.* London: Faber and Faber, Ltd., 1951.

Paris, Pierre. *Goya.* Paris: Librairie Plon, 1928.

Poore, Charles Craydon. *Goya.* London and New York, Charles Scribner's Sons, 1938.

Rich, Daniel Catton, ed. *The Art of Goya,* with a note on the technique of Goya by F. Schmid. Catalogue. Chicago: The Art Institute of Chicago, 1941.

Royal Academy of Arts. *Goya and His Times.* London: Royal Academy, 1963.

Sánchez Cantón, F. J. *Goya,* tr. by Georges Pillement. Paris: G. Crès & Cie., 1930.

―――. *Goya.* Milan: Rizzoli Editore; New York: Reynald, 1964.

―――. *Vida y Obras de Goya.* Madrid: Editorial Peninsular, 1951.

Sambricio, Valentin. *Francisco Bayeu.* Madrid: Instituto Diego

Velázquez, 1955.

Sedgwick, Henry D. *Spain, a Short History*. Boston: Little, Brown & Co., 1931.

Stokes, Hugh. *Francisco Goya*. New York: G. P. Putnam's Sons, 1914.

Trapier, Elizabeth du Gué. *Goya, a Study of His Portraits, 1797–99*. New York: The Hispanic Society of America, 1955.

———. *Goya and His Sitters*. New York: The Hispanic Society of America, 1964.

Vallentin, Antonina. *This I Saw: The Life and Times of Goya*, tr. by Katherine Woods. New York: Random House, Inc., 1949.

Wehle, Harry B. *Fifty Drawings by Francisco Goya*. New York: The Metropolitan Museum of Art, 1938.

Young, Blamire. *The Proverbs of Goya*. London: Jonathan Cape, 1923.

Yriarte, Charles E. *Goya*. Paris: Plon, 1867.

Zapater y Gómez, Francisco. *Goya: Noticias Biográficas*. Zaragoza: La Perserverencia, 1868.

Articles

Font, Eleanor S. "Goya's Source for the Maragato Series," in *Gazette des Beaux-Arts*. November, 1958.

Grappe, Georges. "Goya dans les Collections de France," in *L'Amour de l'Art*. Paris, Editions Hypérion, No. 1, February, 1938.

———. "Goya, Chant Profond de l'Espagne," in *L'Illustration*. December, 1938.

Reitmann, F. "Goya: A Medical Study," in *Character and Personality*, Vol. VIII, No. 1, September, 1939.

Sambricio, Valentin. "Goya no fue Afrancesado," in *Arriba* (Madrid), March 31, 1946.

Sánchez Cantón, F. J. "Cómo vivía Goya," in *Archivo Español de Arte*, No. 74, April–June, 1946.

Sánchez de Rivera, Daniel. "La Enfermidad de Goya," in *Revista Española de Arte*, anno IV, No. 5, March, 1935.

Trapier, Elizabeth du Gué. "Goya's Portrait of Pedro Mocarte." New York: The Hispanic Society of America, 1959.

———. "Unpublished Drawings by Goya in The Hispanic Society of America." *Master Drawings*, Vol. I, No. 1, spring, 1963.

263

Index

264

265